M000231338

HOW
teens
WIN

HOW
teens
WIN

THE STUDENT'S GUIDE TO
ACCOMPLISHING BIG GOALS

JON ACUFF
WITH L.E. ACUFF
AND McRAE ACUFF

BakerBooks

a division of Baker Publishing Group
Grand Rapids, Michigan

Published by Baker Books
a division of Baker Publishing Group
Grand Rapids, Michigan
BakerBooks.com

Printed in the United States of America

Library of Congress Cataloging-in-Publication Data
Names: Acuff, Jon, author. | Acuff, L.E., author. | Acuff, McRae, author.
Title: How teens win : the student's guide to accomplishing big goals / Jon
    Acuff with L.E. Acuff and McRae Acuff.
Description: Grand Rapids, Michigan : Baker Books, [2024] | Includes
    bibliographical references. | Audience: Ages 14–17
Identifiers: LCCN 2023053355 | ISBN 9781540903822 (paperback) | ISBN
    9781540904478 (casebound) | ISBN 9781493446988 (ebook)
Subjects: LCSH: Goal (Psychology)—Juvenile literature. | Motivation
    (Psychology) in adolescence—Juvenile literature. | Students—Conduct
    of life—Juvenile literature. | Teenagers—Conduct of life—Juvenile literature.
Classification: LCC BF505.G6 .A334 2024 | DDC 158.10835—dc23/
    eng/20240213
LC record available at https://lccn.loc.gov/2023053355

Interior design by William Overbeeke
Cover design by Faceout Studio, Amanda Hudson

Published in association with Yates & Yates, www.yates2.com.

Baker Publishing Group publications use paper produced from sustainable forestry practices and postconsumer waste whenever possible.

24 25 26 27 28 29 30   7 6 5 4 3 2 1

To every teacher, coach, youth worker,
parent, and grandparent
who gave a student *Your New Playlist*
and told us to write another book—
thank you for the encouragement.
Here it is!

L.E., McRae, and Jon

CONTENTS

INTRODUCTION

I didn't peak in high school.

I did whatever is the opposite of peak.

My freshman year got off to a disastrous start. That fall our basketball team went 0 for 18. All my friends got called up to varsity, but at five foot seven I was definitely not even going to crack JV. I fouled out of most games because there were only seven people on the team and nobody would play defense except me.

I didn't have a single date all year, which is weird because I shaved stripes into my eyebrow to look more like "Ice Ice Baby" rapper Vanilla Ice (ask your parents), so I'm not sure what the issue was.

I got a D+ on my History Day project, a school-wide event where students spend weeks preparing presentations on topics like the US Constitution,

Paul Revere's ride, and the Magna Carta. My project was titled "The History of Rap," which at that point in 1991 was about 15 minutes old. I stood there grinning like a fool next to a hastily thrown together collage of photos of Run DMC and Public Enemy.

My grades continued to crater until my parents suggested I might be a better fit for an all-boys Catholic high school four towns over. I didn't fully understand what a big change that would be. The teachers are Xaverian Brothers who wear robes? I have to wear a sport coat and tie every day? What was that last part about no girls? I had a lot of questions but was quickly running out of options as a failing freshman, so I transferred.

I'd roller-coaster through the next few years having random ups and downs.

Cut from the soccer team? Down.

Won the school poetry contest? Up.

Got serious about tap dancing? Eh, that one is hard to call, but I doubt that right now you're thinking, "Man, this guy did poetry AND tap dancing? He's the coolest!"

The Next Thirty Years

If you're expecting a comeback story in college, I'm about to disappoint you. Those four years had their own issues. Please refer to my "rave phase" and the failed Halloween prank of 1994. Did you know that when you set off a fire extinguisher inside someone's dorm room it also sets off the fire alarm and empties a 400-person building at 2 a.m.? You do now.

I wouldn't turn things around until my mid-30s when I started to figure out who I wanted to be. I'm what people call a "late bloomer." It took me forever to get it together.

Looking back on my middle school and high school years once I was older, there was a question I started to think about often:

What advice would you give your younger self?

I'm 48 years old right now. If I could go back in time and talk to 12-year-old me or 17-year-old me, what would I say? What hope would I give him? What secrets would I bestow on him that would make the next 30 years so much easier and more enjoyable?

The short answer is, "You don't have to wait to be awesome. You can be awesome right now."

The long answer is this book.

I waited until my 30s to figure out some goals, decide who I am, and build the life I wanted. I stumbled through decades of bad decisions, dumb decisions, and no decisions, but if you remember only one thing from this book, remember this: I didn't have to. You don't either.

You can peak in high school.

You can also peak in college.

You can then peak in your 20s and your 30s, and while you might not believe for a second that you'll actually ever be this ancient, you can even peak in your 40s too.

You can have a good life that progressively gets better every day.

I tell your parents this all the time because they have a hard time believing it too.

We did a study where we asked more than 3,000 adults if they felt like they were living up to their full potential. We were surprised to find that 50 percent of those surveyed said 50 percent of their full potential is untapped.

Imagine if every Christmas you only opened up half your gifts. You could see the rest—there was a whole pile of them in the corner of the room—but you never got to them. The crazy thing is that no one was stopping you. There might even be friends, family members, teachers, or coaches encouraging you to open them all, but for some reason they just felt out of reach.

Would that make for a happy Christmas, a happy house, a happy senior year, a happy anything? Of course not, but it doesn't have to be that way. You can start opening every gift right now.

I Needed This Book in High School, but I Can't Write It Today

If I could go back in time, I'd give this book to that freshman me with the striped eyebrow.

I'd tell him that if he only did 10 percent of what's inside these pages, the next 20 years of his life would be way more amazing and way less messy. I can't though. Try as I might, there's no *Back to the Future* Delorean in my driveway. But I can give you this book, and I know it will help because I didn't even write it. Two of your fellow teenagers did.

I mean, just look at my references. I've mentioned Vanilla Ice, Run DMC, and *Back to the Future* in just the introduction. I'm closer to retirement age than I am to high school age. Although I've been where you are, I'm not there anymore.

My two teenage daughters are though. At the time we're writing this, McRae is a senior in high school. L.E. is a sophomore in college. They're in the same halls you are, using the same lockers, trying to figure out the same opportunities and challenges. They're not waiting until later to be awesome—to be honest, they probably wouldn't even use that word. I'm so basic. Or is it mid? Should I be extra? Do I have rizz? Who can keep up?

See? This is why I didn't write the rest of this

book. L.E. and McRae are building goals, launching adventures, and learning what it means to make the most of modern adolescence. You can too.

The best part is you have the greatest gift of all: time. Being young is like being a billionaire in the one resource every adult wishes they had. You make Harry Styles, Steph Curry, and Taylor Swift look poor when it comes to time. What will you do with yours? How will you spend it? Who will you become? How will you win? We're about to find out.

Please just promise me that if you ever run into a short, winless point guard making questionable facial hair decisions, you'll pass on a message. Tell him, "You don't have to wait to be awesome. You can be awesome right now."

The Future Is Ours

There are two questions every teenager has said in school at least once in their lives:

1. Will this be on the test?
2. Will I ever use this later in life?

Both questions drive our teachers crazy, but they matter a lot to us because what we're really asking is simple:

1. Is this important today?
2. Will this be important later?

Do I need to know the political implications of the Suez Canal in order to pass this test?

And when I'm in my 20s or 30s, will anyone ever ask me, "Can you please explain the political implications of the Suez Canal?" If you're a parent reading this right now, be honest—no one at any dinner party you've ever attended has said, "So, tell me a little about your expertise with the Suez Canal."

My name is L.E. Acuff, and if you're a teenager like me reading this, you've got enough other school books to finish, so let's keep this "bonus book" short and sweet by quickly answering both questions.

No, nothing inside this book will be on the test because there is no test.

More than likely, a parent or grandparent gave you this book and said, "Here, I think you might like this."

They gave it to you for a very simple reason: they wish they had read it when they were our age. Our parents have a hard time explaining this to us, but they're kind of like time machines. They've been to the future we're headed to and have come back with a few tips. They've made some mistakes, gotten some bruises, and overpaid for lessons that they hope we can learn a lot quicker.

They've been to their 20s, 30s, 40s, or beyond and have returned with ideas they wish they knew when they were our age. In addition to advice at dinner or wise words while dropping you off for school, they've given you this book.

But no, there is no test. I promise.

The answer to the second question is exactly the opposite.

Will you need to know this later in life?

Yes. A thousand times yes.

Inside these pages is a treasure map to the very best treasure you'll ever discover—yourself.

Your potential.

Your possibility.

Your biggest goals.

Your future.

It's all waiting for you just beyond the next page. I dare you to read it and see what happens next.

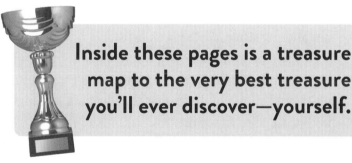

Inside these pages is a treasure map to the very best treasure you'll ever discover—yourself.

The Best Moments List

I (L.E.) love lists!

I like cliffhangers too, and the last chapter was a bit of one. But even more than a "to be continued" moment in a show or book, I love a good list.

That makes sense, though, because I'm an accountant and my sister McRae is an artist.

Or I will be eventually. Right now I'm a sophomore in college, which means I have two years left to figure out this major. But so far the business school has been a good fit for me.

In high school, I played trumpet in the marching band. I liked the hidden math in all the notes, which is probably why I also played piano, acoustic guitar, and even ukulele. I didn't regularly play the recorder because that is a musical torture device they force on elementary school children to make parents frustrated as you wail away on it in the car rider line. Has anyone ever played the recorder well?

Marching band appealed to me because in addition to the sheet music, there was so much mathematical precision required to move 200 high school students across a football field under the stadium lights. I liked that we all had charts and "dots" that told us where to stand at any given moment. There were lists upon lists in high school band.

I still enjoy details like that. Just ask the 19 other girls who came to a spring break trip I planned with my sorority sisters. Have you ever organized seven days of meals for 20 college students? Do you know how many carts that takes at Costco? Do you know how many bags of chips, bottles of ranch dressing, and cases of LaCroix that is? Or how best to divide the bedrooms to minimize the drama while maximizing the fun? Do you know how many slides you need in a slideshow you send out a month before the trip to make sure everyone pays their deposit, arrives on time, and leaves happy?

I do. I listed and charted and diagrammed that entire thing like I was landing a rocket on Mars. And I loved every moment of it.

I was tired at the end of the week—19 people is a lot for an introvert like me—but it was worth it.

That's another obvious difference between McRae and me: she's an extrovert, I'm an introvert. Throughout this book, we'll point out those differences between us because it's a great reminder that everyone reading this has their own unique personality, strengths, weaknesses, opportunities, and challenges.

We'd never want to assume that you're just like us, so the stories, ideas, and advice we'll share are pulled from students of all ages, life experiences, and outlooks. Despite the many things that make us all different, we're going to start in the same place: the List. Its full name is the Best Moments List, but "the List" sounded more dramatic in the moment.

I'll let McRae explain it because we're only a few pages in and I'm already hogging the mic.

Everyone Gets an A on This Project

My name is McRae, I'm 18 years old, and I'm a senior in high school. I like cross-country, *The Office*, and collaging until I run out of paint. I also don't know what I want to be when I grow up. Not exactly anyway. If you don't either, you're in the right place. If your parents are at all concerned that you don't know what you want to do after high school, feel free to say, "One of the authors in the book you gave me doesn't even know either, Mom."

The good news, for both of us, is that there are a few easy tricks you can do to start taking steps in the right direction. It's like turning on the first light in a pitch-black room. It doesn't clear every shadow, but it does make the room dramatically easier to navigate. It also gives you enough light to see the next switch you need to flip on.

Sometimes, being a teenager feels like learning to drive a car in the middle of a storm. You can't see exactly where you're going, but if you look hard enough, you can just make out the speed limit sign, the white line in the middle of the road, and all the cars around. The farther you drive, the more comfortable you get with the windshield wipers, the deep puddles you have to navigate, and the pace of the traffic. Before you know it, you're back in your driveway and you've navigated prom. Or getting cut from a team. Or how to respond to a mean text.

Our age would be easy if there was only one storm we had to drive through. But there are more than you think, which is why the Best Moments List is so helpful.

How easy is this to use?

Easier than my English quiz on the impact of federal tax dollars in school systems. If that feels oddly specific, it's only because my dad recently helped me take that exact quiz—and we failed.

A few months ago, I missed a week of school because I was sick. That created a homework hole that was difficult to dig out of. My dad helped me catch up and even promised that we'd work on my English quiz together. He had to retire from math help when I was in about the fourth grade. As soon as I hit fractions he said, "I love you, but your mom is right over there. You better ask her."

He's a writer, though, so I assumed that an English 3 quiz would be right up his alley. Before we submitted the quiz answers online for our grade, he apologized and said, "I think we may have missed one. I bet we got a 7 out of 8, which isn't so bad." I hit Submit and the screen refreshed.

We got 4 out of 8.

If you're bad at math too, that's a 50 percent.

My dad wrote my English teacher a long email explaining why so many of the questions could have gone multiple ways. He was flabbergasted at the grade and was certain he could get us some extra points if he just explained the situation properly.

The answer was "no."

The F stood.

That quiz was impossible.

The Best Moments List though? This is going to be easy.

It's not even a quiz.

It's an invitation.

You can't fail it.

You can't underperform it.

You can't blow it.

You can only build it.

And when you do, you're going to know the most important person in your life a whole lot better—yourself.

How to Build a Best Moments List

There are only two steps to building a Best Moments List:

1. Write down your best moments.
2. Repeat.

That's it. That's all it takes to start a Best Moments List. We told you it was easy.

Why are we going to create one? Because when you know what you care about, every decision in life gets easier.

Although my dad is apparently pretty average at English, he's a lot better at exercises like this. He should be—he wrote a whole book for adults about Best Moments Lists. He created it because he

When you know **WHAT YOU CARE ABOUT,** every decision in life gets **EASIER.**

JON ACUFF   #HowTeensWin

noticed adults feeling overwhelmed trying to figure out what they want to do with the rest of their lives.

Has anyone ever asked you, "What do you want to be when you grow up?" Guess what? Adults get asked that question too, and it's as hard for them to answer as it is for us. So my dad built a different way to turn potential into a goal and then took thousands and thousands of people through this exercise. The only difference is that he was teaching people in their 30s, 40s, 50s, and 60s. He was showing them how to review their past so they could enjoy their present and prepare their future.

That works when you've been on the planet for a few decades and have a lot of past to review, but our approach is going to be a little different. If you want to take a spin down memory lane and the last five years of your life, feel free, but the greater lessons when you're our age will come from your present, not your past.

If we learn how to pay attention to what lights us up today, we can custom build the kind of tomorrow we really want.

You know how much you love being part of the robotics club? Imagine if you could identify what you really enjoy about that experience. You'd have an amazing clue to help you shape your senior year of high school, college, or even—and I know this feels like a long way off—your career.

That's the goal of the Best Moments List. It tells you who you are so you can start becoming who you really want to be.

I (McRae) will go first since I'm the one typing right now. Here are a few things that belong on my own Best Moments List:

1. Going to Sonic with my friend Ann, even though they stopped serving cookie dough (as if Heath Bar is a suitable replacement).
2. Listening to music in my room by myself.
3. Putting together puzzles, preferably 750 pieces.
4. Doing paint by numbers. (Anyone can look like an expert!)
5. Seeing Taylor Swift in concert.
6. Reading and then rereading the Harry Potter series.
7. Knowing the time. That's a small one, but it's true. I feel lost without my watch.
8. AP US History. I'm a history nerd.
9. Walking across the street and spending a few hours at my friend Kate's house.
10. Babysitting.
11. When L.E. comes home from college and all her friends visit us.

12. Taking and teaching art lessons in an after-school program.

13. My 2002 Toyota 4Runner with 198,000 miles on it. It's a little beat-up, the radio doesn't work, and there's a taillight out, but it's mine.

14. Calling my grandmother Mimi for quick conversations.

15. Spending a week with my grandmother Lolly in the summer.

That's just a snippet of a list, and it was incredibly easy to come up with.

I'd freeze if you asked me, "Who are you, McRae? What are your lifelong aspirations? What do you want to be when you grow up?" Those kinds of questions are too big, too undefined, and too hard to answer. "What do you like?" is a lot easier to answer and a lot more fun to think about.

I personally think you should talk your parents into paying you a quarter per item you write down. I could have made $25 from my list of 100. (I just shared the first 15 items in this chapter.)

If you'd like to get your list going—which, again, is the fastest, easiest, funnest way to introduce you to you—let's talk about a few questions that will help you get started.

The Questions

If I (L.E.) give my dad a short answer to a question, I run the risk of an impromptu dance party.

For example, if we're in a grocery store together on a Saturday and he asks, "What do you want to do after this?" it helps to have an answer other than "I don't know." If I say that, he will immediately respond with, "We could always just have a dance party!"

There, in the frozen food section, he will start dancing in the most dad way possible, which is to say terribly. It's an excruciating display I will do just about anything to avoid. If you answer the questions I'm about to ask with "I don't know," I don't think my dad will come to your town and dance, but he might. He has a lot of frequent-flier miles.

That's the risk you run, but you also run the risk of missing out on a life-changing activity.

It's faster than becoming an Eagle Scout, cheaper than seeing your favorite musician in concert, and might just be something you never forget. And it all starts with a few simple questions.

1. What is your favorite class of all time?

I don't mean your favorite class just this year, I mean of all the classes you've ever had. If you want to write down your first-grade class, go for it. If you took environmental science sophomore year and fell in love, put it down.

If it's more of a subject you love, like English, instead of a specific class, write that down. If you can't think of any, if you go 0 for whatever grade you're in right now, ask yourself a different question.

What class do you wish your school offered?

Would you do anything for an automotive class where you could work on your own rarely running 1992 Nissan 300ZX, which your mom said you shouldn't buy and now sits dead in your driveway? Add that to your list. Think of this first question as exploring the best of what was, what is, and what could be.

2. What is your favorite part of your favorite class?

Let's get a little more specific. What did you really like about that class? What made it special?

McRae might put her kindergarten class on her list, and the reason why is simple: Mrs. Robinson. She was an elementary school legend, and she certainly taught my sister a lot. But McRae's favorite thing is that on Fridays, if the class had behaved all week, Mrs. Robinson would get on the table and dance. (She was way better at dancing than my dad.)

I could list fifth grade with Mr. Caruso. One of the best things is that he would stand at the door to the class and shake everyone's hand before they came into the room. It was such an official start to the day, and that small gesture meant a lot to me.

So, what was your favorite part of your favorite class?

3. What makes you jealous on social media?

Ooh, curveball. When you're on TikTok, Snapchat, or Instagram, what does someone else have that you wish you had? Be honest. There's no need to clean up your answer. McRae once got excluded from a birthday party that all her friends went to, and seeing it on Instagram hurt her feelings.

She'd put that on her list not because it was a favorite moment but because of what it says about her. She wants community. She wants to be included. She cares about relationships. She values people. If she pays attention to that feeling, then she can make sure that she puts a priority on staying connected to friends in the future.

Maybe for you it's stuff. Do you wish you had the gaming setup a friend posted about? Is there a Lululemon item you keep eyeing on somebody else's Snapchat? Is it a car? Do you feel like you're the only one in your grade who doesn't have one and your classmate's new Mustang drives you nuts?

Maybe it's a trip. There was a girl I went to high school with who attended 12 Harry Styles concerts. I don't just mean in America either. She flew to London to catch him live.

Maybe it's an achievement. Someone you know posted their 30 on the ACT and suddenly your 22 looks very small.

Should you wallow in social media frustration? No. Long-term jealousy only causes long-term harm, but pay attention to those moments when you feel a bit of it bubble up. Your heart might be trying to send you a small message in a bottle about the things that are important to you.

4. What adult has the kind of life you'd want?

That might feel like an unusual question, but I promise it's a helpful one. Is there a cousin you look up to? She moved to New York after graduating from law school and is a public defender helping people who can't afford lawyers. You love seeing her Instagram updates with photos of small, interesting restaurants in Brooklyn. At Thanksgiving, even though she's 15 years older than you, she tells you stories about her cases like you're a peer. Write her name down on your list.

Maybe there's a coach who inspires you. He turned his passion for football into his whole career and that seems like something you want to do too.

Maybe there's a neighbor with an old-school Bronco, a dog that's cool, and a boat. "Check, check, check," you think as you dream about your own life.

What adult has the kind of life you'd want?

You don't have to ask any of these people to mentor you—let's not get too wild since this is only the third chapter. But when you think about the adults you know, who has the kind of life you want?

You'd be surprised how many students like us find their careers without even knowing it when we bump into the right adult who shows us a picture of what the future could look like.

5. What's a hobby, sport, club, or after-school activity you like?

We talked a little about what you like inside of school, but what about outside?

Are you on the mountain bike team? (Do you wish your school had a mountain bike team?) Have you reread the Hunger Games series a dozen times? Do you eat, sleep, and breathe volleyball? Do you have a LEGO closet with the entire Star Wars universe in it? Are you a musician, gamer, athlete, or anything else?

When you have free time, where does it go? This is an important question because our generation has the unique ability to turn hobbies into careers. Take gaming for instance. You know that "bad habit" your grandmother was worried about? You can get a scholarship to college for that! You can become an e-sports athlete and make a living on Twitch where other people pay money to watch you do what you love.

I know a student who turned a hobby into a career in my hometown. His hobby was overnight oats. Does that feel too obscure to be a life-changing passion? Tell that to his 2.3 million followers on TikTok who love his funny recipe videos. He's built a massive following that's making so much money, he dropped out of college to focus on it. He started with oatmeal and is now a 19-year-old CEO of his own food brand. Twenty years ago that would have been impossible.

If this one is challenging for you to answer, just fill in the blank: "This is weird, but I like _____."

What's the weirdest thing you like? As artist James Victore says, "The things that made you weird as a kid make you great today." He's talking to adults of course, but is there a weird interest that might hold the secret to a long-term interest for you?

My mom, Jenny, used to play project manager in her closet when she was a kid. She asked for office supplies for Christmas. Who wants Post-it Notes in their stocking? My mom did. What was her first job after grad school? She was a project manager for a construction company.

My dad, Jon, used to scribble poetry down in the third grade. None of his friends were passing their weekends that way. That was a little weird. What does he do for a job today? He writes books.

Don't be afraid to be a little weird. There might be something wonderful hidden there.

6. Every time I see _____, I smile.

Let's end this exercise with three fill in the blanks, something you're probably very familiar with from schoolwork.

This one is fun because the answer can be anything. You could write down a friend's name. When I see my friend Jadyn unexpectedly on campus, I smile. It's automatic and instant. It could be a place. When you see your bedroom, especially after a stressful day, you smile. It could be a pet. Maybe your cat is your best friend and when you see him jump on the couch to curl into your lap, you smile.

It could be an object. You love your kayak. Your dad gave it to you and you get an instant sense of adventure every time you see it hanging on the fence in your backyard. It could be a race bib from your first 5K or maybe a record player. You know it would be easier to listen to Spotify, but a vinyl album feels different and special to you.

The next time you smile, pay attention to what made you do it.

7. When I scroll through the photos on my phone, I always get inspired when I see
_____.

At some point, you cared about a moment enough to take a photo. Take a walk through the past and see what you captured. You could do the same thing on Instagram. You might think you remember those hundreds or even thousands of snapshots, but I bet you've forgotten a few.

The digital records we keep become clues to the things that matter to us. If any of the other prompts felt time-consuming, this one is super easy. Chances are you've already done this a few times when you were bored.

This time go through it with a purpose.

8. I could spend hours talking about _____.

Maybe you don't consider yourself an expert but there's a topic you can't stop talking about. My friend Sarah talks constantly about photography. She built a small side hustle with her camera and is quick to tell you all about the senior portrait sessions she's got lined up. My friend Judge will talk your ear off about working out. My friend Colton will share all the reasons this is a great time for teenagers to get involved in local activism.

Those are three very different ways to fill in this blank, but you can put anything down. Don't limit yourself.

What could you talk about for hours?

What Happens Next

Those are just eight suggestions, but there are countless ways you can work on your own Best Moments List. When you do, something surprising is going to happen—three things, actually.

The first is that you will feel amazing. How could you not? You've just asked your head and your heart to google up a huge collection of your favorite moments. Doesn't it sometimes feel like those two parts of us do the opposite? Has a random thought about something dumb you said or did ever knocked you over unexpectedly? In the middle of class your brain says, "I can't believe you said that at lunch last week. What were you thinking?!"

That happens to all of us, but now we're doing the opposite. We're not just hoping a good memory will find us—we're on the hunt for it. And the more you list, the better you'll feel.

The second surprise is that you'll start to feel grateful. Even if you only write down five things, seeing those five things will make you thankful. A friend's name, a vacation you loved, a song that makes you happy—as you walk through your list, you'll have a sense of gratitude for the things you do have. Social media is a fantastic source for feeling like you're lacking, but this list does the opposite. It's a gratitude machine.

The third surprise is that you'll gain a little bit of self-awareness. That's a big phrase for "knowing yourself." We're growing and changing and shifting so quickly as teenagers that some days it feels impossible to get ahold of who we really are.

When my dad was a freshman in high school, his mom said to him one night after a homework battle, "It's like you're two different people." He was either really studious, turning in every assignment with precision and thoughtfulness, or completely unplugged and prone to failing classes. He didn't know who he was or what he wanted to be.

He didn't have a Best Moments List to say, "Here, these are the things that you like, the things that make you feel like you."

But you have that. And if you spend a little time with it, you'll learn some unexpected things about yourself.

Those three things alone—happiness, gratitude, and self-awareness—would be worth the price of the book, but they're just the tip of the iceberg. Once you have a Best Moments List built on what you love today, you have everything you need to plan your best tomorrow.

Label What You Love

Have you ever been to Universal Studios in Orlando? I (McRae) went for the first time a few months ago. As a massive Harry Potter fan, I was excited to experience the Hogwarts and Hogsmeade sections of the park.

We got there early because it was a Saturday during spring break season and we were anticipating a large crowd. My mom loves Disney World, and it was killing her a little bit inside that we weren't at the Magic Kingdom.

Actually, I think what was bothering her was that she wasn't going to be able to "win the day." She has Disney down to a science. She knows those parks like the back of her hand. From ensuring we're there in the morning when Mickey Mouse arrives on the train to open the Magic Kingdom to bringing just the right amount of snacks from home so we can save money on "exorbitant turkey legs," her competitive spirit comes through even at a child's theme park. I bet at least one of your parents is the same way. Gotta have a plan, people!

Standing in line, I was amazed to see how many other teenagers were dressed up for the moment. A girl near me had her hair bun held up by wands. Several fans were dressed in full quidditch uniforms, and others were wearing long, black robes representing the different houses like Gryffindor and even Slytherin. I didn't see a lot of Hufflepuff memorabilia, which is probably because the Sorting Hat throws that house right under the (knight) bus. Gryffindor is brave. Slytherin is cunning. Ravenclaw is wise. "Good Hufflepuff, she took the rest." Rough.

As we jostled for a better spot in line, the excitement built until they finally opened the gates. Because we'd never been to Universal Studios before, we didn't really know where to run first. So we just followed the crowds.

A mass of people led us past the Hulk roller coaster, through Seuss Landing, and finally to Hogsmeade. In a matter of minutes, the line for

Hagrid's Magical Creatures Motorbike Adventure jumped to a 250-minute wait time.

Fortunately, in that rare instance, the crowd steered us the right direction, but that's not always what happens when you follow what everyone else is doing. That's what high school feels like sometimes. You don't know where you're headed, so you just chase after what everyone else is chasing. But high school and Hogwarts are a lot easier to navigate if you have your own map and can make your own decisions for your own life.

That's what I'm about to show you with the Best Moments List. There's a map inside it, and it's even easier to follow than the Marauder's Map.

Categories and Clues

There are a few motivational statements all parents like to say. Favorites include:

"It doesn't matter if you win or lose as long as you tried your best."

"Shoot for the moon. Even if you miss, you'll land among the stars."

"If life gives you lemons, make lemonade."

I bet your parents have said similar things to you. One that my parents love is "You get out what you put in." That one is particularly annoying because it's true. If I run more in the summer, I have a better cross-country season in the fall. If I take practice ACTs before the real test, the real test feels a lot better. If I reach out to my friends more often, I have better relationships.

You get out what you put in.

So many things in life work on that principle, and the Best Moments List certainly does too. The more items you list, the better you'll know who you are today. The better you know who you are today, the better equipped you'll be to end up where you want to be tomorrow.

It's like adding more details to a map so that it's easier to use. If you've got 10 best moments on your list, awesome. If you've got 30 on your list, awesomer. The longer the list, the better the map. There's not an exact number you need, but a sprint to 30 is often a good place to start. If you can get 30 items down—which is $7.50 if you convince your parents to pay you a quarter each—you've got more than enough to notice the patterns that are always there.

I don't know exactly what's on your list, but I do

The better you
know who you are
TODAY,
the better equipped
you'll be to end up
where you
want to be
TOMORROW.

JON ACUFF

#HowTeensWin

know that every single moment will fit into one of four categories:

1. Experiences
2. Wins
3. Relationships
4. Stuff

Those four categories have been secretly driving the best parts of your life for years. But what do they mean?

Experience = A best moment you took part in.

It could be an experience that only happened once, like going to Universal Studios. It could be an experience that happens often, like going to your favorite store such as Lululemon, Academy Sports, or Bass Pro. It could be a massive moment like getting invited to prom or something as small as putting together a puzzle one afternoon. Simply put, it's an experience you enjoyed.

Win = A best moment achieved through your effort.

This is a task or a goal you succeeded at. Passing calculus is a win. Getting your driver's license is a win. Making the varsity soccer team is a win.

Receiving a scholarship to college is a win. Going to Universal Studios was an experience, but for me it wasn't a win. I didn't pay for the tickets with money I saved up from babysitting. My dad paid for everything because he is incredibly generous and occasionally will try to add sentences like this one to the book. If I rode more roller coasters than I ever had before, setting a new personal record, that would be a win, but just going was an experience.

Relationship = A moment another person made best.

This is the easiest one to identify because if there's another person involved, it's a relationship moment. If you removed that person, the moment wouldn't make the list. For example, going on a run with my friends is a best moment. I love catching up with them. But if they weren't there, I wouldn't consider that a best moment. You might not love practice, but you enjoy the friends you get to run laps with, so even that can become a best moment because of the relationship.

Stuff = A physical object you think is the best.

This fourth category is slightly different from the first three, but it's every bit as important. This is a physical object that makes you happy. It could be your old, beat-up car. It has a million miles, the back windows don't roll down, and the trunk smells like wet dog, but it represents so much more to you than just a used Toyota Corolla. Ask any adult and they will tell you, everyone remembers their first car. That's the stuff life is made of. It can be a well-loved T-shirt or a baseball glove, a pocketknife or a video game. It can be a weighted blanket that makes you feel safe or a lift kit on a Jeep that makes you feel dangerous. It all counts.

Experiences, wins, relationships, and stuff—I bet some new ideas came to mind just reading those descriptions. Write those down too! You don't just build a Best Moments List once. You can add to it as often as you like. Next, take a quick look at your list. Which categories jump out at you?

Why does understanding the categories matter so much? Because when you do, you don't have to guess who you are or what you care about—you actually have a snapshot that tells you. It's like finally seeing the individual ingredients for your favorite meal and then realizing you can cook it again and again.

The fun thing is that every single adult you know wishes they had done this exercise at our age. How do I know? Because my dad has told me about "the ladder problem" a million times.

One Reason Adults Are So Grumpy

There's an analogy people use to describe what it feels like when you chase the wrong goal for a few years. They say it's like putting your ladder against the wrong wall. This is what happens when someone in their mid-30s wakes up and realizes they don't like their job.

They maybe knew that a little bit in college. Their major didn't suit their personality or their skills, but it was a safe choice. In their 20s, they didn't love being in that particular industry, but they wanted to use the major they'd paid so much for, so they kept climbing the ladder.

Ten years later, they open their eyes and discover they've put their ladder against the wrong wall. They don't want to be up there, but it feels too late to change. They've been climbing up rung after rung since they were our age, and switching walls feels overwhelming.

That's what happened to my dad when he was 34. He woke up one day and realized he was at the top of a ladder called "senior content designer" and didn't want to be there. Worst of all, there were no more rungs. He couldn't become a "super senior content designer." He'd reached the end of a ladder that was against the wrong wall and had to completely change his career.

This is why grumpy adults at family gatherings will often pull us aside and say things like "Never grow up, kid—it's a trap."

It's not though. Never take advice from a frustrated adult who doesn't like the way their life turned out. Being an adult can be amazing. Fourteen years after he got stuck, my dad has written 10 books, traveled from Portugal to Greece to Hawaii for speaking events, and fallen in love with a life he couldn't have possibly imagined when he was stuck on that ladder.

But like he said in the introduction to this book, you and I don't have to wait to do any of that. We can start right now, and we already have with our Best Moments Lists.

Simple Math, Super Life

Has a teacher ever taught you the difference between *show* and *tell*?

We often linked them together in kindergarten when we'd bring in something fun from home to share with the class, but they're actually two completely different approaches to education. One is a lot more effective than the other.

When you *tell* someone how to do something, it's a lecture. You use words and little else as you describe something the student can't see. When you *show* a student the lesson, the experience comes alive in fresh ways.

You don't *tell* them about a scientific principle, waving your hands about as if trying to mime what a beaker looks like. You *show* them what happens when you break apart the covalent bonds between hydrogen atoms and oxygen atoms using an actual beaker, water, salt, alligator clips, and a 9-volt battery.

Which would you understand quicker and remember longer—being told about the experiment or shown the experiment? The answer is obvious, so instead of just telling you about the categories for your Best Moments List, let me (L.E.) show you a few examples from real teenagers.

Working at Discount Tire = Win

Emmett Foss is a junior at Franklin High School in Franklin, Tennessee. One of the things he'd put on his Best Moments List is his after-school job at Discount Tire. Why does he love it? Well, he's a car guy, so repairing tire issues is a lot of fun. There's also a relationship aspect because he likes the people he works with. But ultimately, this is a win because Emmett has to accomplish a lot to make this job successful. He has to get himself to work on time. That's a win. The company has a standard of excellence they expect him to meet. That's a win. He has to manage his schedule and balance his schoolwork. That's a win. He gets paid. That's a win. Every tire he replaces is a small, round win that makes the hours

Work and school are full of wins if you know how to spot them.

of his job fly by. Work and school are full of wins if you know how to spot them.

Being a member of the high school color guard = Relationship

Lawren Williams, a senior, loves being on the color guard. There are definitely a few wins involved, like the solo she had in last year's *I Love Lucy* performance. And performing in Grand Nationals at Lucas Oil Stadium, home of the Indianapolis Colts, was the definition of an experience. But ultimately this is a relationship moment. Why? Because if you removed everyone else from this story, it wouldn't make her list. In fact, it wouldn't even happen. Without 200 other people, it would just be Lawren standing alone on a football field and awkwardly holding a flag. It's the other people who make it special. It's the teamwork that makes it meaningful. It's the friendships that make it memorable. The color guard doesn't just practice together 20 hours a week. They eat lunch together. They travel together. They do sleepovers together. This moment is 100 percent relationship.

Putting together the LEGO Atari 2600 set = Experience

Blaze D'melio, a senior at Centennial High School, is going to engineering school when he graduates. When you see his collection of LEGO sets you'll know why. He loves putting things together—it's just how his mind works. Even if they are vintage items he never experienced the first time they came around, like the Atari set. Blaze never played games like *Centipede* or *Asteroids*. Blaze was negative 25 years old when Atari came out in 1981. He wouldn't be born for another two decades, but he still loved putting together the LEGO model because of the experience. Picking out the set at Target is an experience. Unboxing it is an experience. Sorting all the pieces is an experience. Putting it together all alone for some much-appreciated introvert time is an experience. If he put it together faster than anyone else, that would be a win. If he built it with his friend, that would be a relationship. A LEGO set is definitely stuff, so he could have labeled it that way.

But it's the building experience Blaze loves the most, so this is an experience moment.

Starring in the high school play = Win

Bridget Walker is in a play right now. I don't know when you'll be reading this book, but I know she's in a play somewhere right now regardless of what time of year it is because Bridget Walker is always in a play. By the time she was a freshman in high school, she'd already performed in a dozen different productions. She likes the relationships. She likes the experience. But she LOVES the win. The challenge of it all is what inspires her. Memorizing scripts, learning dance moves, singing beyond her comfort level, making sure her makeup and costume are just right—there are dozens of opportunities for wins in each performance. Maybe for you it's a football game, a robotics build, an AP test, or a speech in Model UN. Chances are, you have some activity that calls you beyond yourself. That's a win.

An Xbox = Stuff

When sophomore Matthew Wood gets in trouble, his mom takes away his Xbox. That's actually a surprising way to immediately find something you should put on your Best Moments List. What do you lose access to when you're grounded?

Is it going with your friends to a concert? That's a relationship moment.

Is it driving yourself to school? Did you get put back on the bus for a week like a senior who shall remain unnamed did in my neighborhood? That's an experience moment.

Is it your Xbox? The latest game? A newer headset? That's all stuff. Stuff is simple to label. Your favorite pair of Jordans is stuff. A baseball hat you wear every day is stuff. Your AirPods are stuff. That Christmas or birthday present you always wanted and finally got is stuff.

If it sounds like it's easy to label your list, that's only because it is. Also, you can't fail at this activity because it's not a test. It's a treasure hunt designed to help you discover what you really value. Objects are easy to label. You won't confuse a favorite pair of jeans with a win. Relationships are simple too. Was there another person in the moment? Then guess what—that's a relationship moment.

Sometimes there's overlap between wins and experiences, but there's an illustration that helps me keep them straight.

Going to a concert by yourself is an experience.

(If that sounds like a weird thing to do, you've never tried to buy Taylor Swift tickets.) If you go to the concert with a friend or a group of friends, that's a relationship. If you paid for the tickets with money you earned from a part-time job, that's a win. If you bought a T-shirt so you'll always remember that night, that's stuff.

To label your list, you don't even have to write out the whole word. Just go through it and put E, W, R, or S beside each item, then add them up. When I did that, my list broke down like this:

40 Wins
28 Relationships
26 Experiences
20 Stuff

McRae's list was a little different:

38 Experiences
32 Relationships
25 Wins
20 Stuff

We had the same number of items in the stuff category, but the other categories were flip-flopped. What did that mean?

Lessons from the List

I dropped my phone in a toilet when I was in the eighth grade.

If you've never had that exact same experience, the first two words you think as it sinks to the bottom of that porcelain prison are "Now what?"

That phrase hits you like a freight train.

Now what?

Do you grab it immediately?

Do you flush first?

Do you look for a plunger to scoop it out?

Do you call for help from the stall next to you?

What do you tell your parents when you get home? "You know how you always tell me to be careful about bringing my phone into the bathroom? Well, funny story . . ."

Will rice save it?

Will you have to get a flip phone as punishment?

Did you just lose all your photos?

A million questions pop into your head, but they all stem from that first one: *Now what?* That's a phrase we hear and feel a lot as teenagers.

You finished eighth grade and are headed to high school. Now what?

You didn't make the lacrosse team. Now what?

You got the score you wanted on the ACT. Now what?

You didn't get invited to the party all your friends went to. Now what?

You got your driver's license. Now what?

You say that phrase a million times when you're our age, but this isn't one of them. If you put together a Best Moments List, you don't have to guess what happens next. I'll tell you. There are four lessons you'll learn immediately.

Lesson 1: There's always a winner.

Hundreds of people have built a Best Moments List and you know what has never happened? There's never been a tie. No one has ever said, "I got 25 wins, 25 relationships, 25 experience moments, and 25 examples of stuff." That's just not the way it works.

There's always a winner. What you love the most is always obvious. For me (L.E.) it was wins. This was not a surprise to anyone. I'm a detail-oriented, driven person. I'm not loud about it. I'm an introvert, but behind the scenes I am working as hard as I can to win. What am I trying to win? Whatever is at stake.

Why did I take six practice ACTs during the summer? Why did I work my way up from almost not making the high school band as a freshman to section leader my senior year? Why did I high point in the Nashville city swim meet? Wins fire me up even if I'm the only one who knows I'm playing a game. I didn't win any public awards for making a Rainbow Loom skirt out of 20,000 rubber bands. It weighed 11 pounds and took me months to finish. But I accomplished it and that's what matters to me.

At any point in that last paragraph did you think to yourself, "Ugh, what a nerd"? McRae would agree with you. She's here for the experience and is motivated very differently than I am. That's one of the reasons it's sometimes hard to get along with your parents. If your dad is a win person and you're a relationship person, he might have a hard time understanding why you're more focused on who you sit with at lunch than what you got on a chemistry exam. It's not that he's right and you're wrong. You just care about different best moments.

For McRae, it's experiences. What does that look like? One example is her summer job. She spent last July volunteering at Camp Crestridge in Black Mountain, North Carolina. For four weeks she washed dishes, picked up trash, and served as a leader-in-training for a camp full of girls ages 7 to 17. What did she make? $0. In fact, my parents had to pay for her to work there.

It wasn't a financial win by any means, but that wasn't the point. The point was the experience. The point was waking up early each morning in the mountains. The point was learning a dozen new skills. The point was walking back to your cabin after encouraging a third-grade camper who might have been a little homesick. The experience mattered most.

Lesson 2: Relationships change a lot when you're a teenager.

When I was in the fifth grade, there were two friends I spent every recess with. We ate lunch together. We hung out together in class. We did jump rope club together. We were inseparable.

A year later, when we were all in middle school, we barely spoke to each other. What happened? Nothing.

When we got to a bigger school with more clubs, sports, and activities, we all just took different paths. There was no fight. There was no falling out. There was no drama. My parents kept asking, "Are you mad at Amanda?" I'd try to explain to them, "No, we just don't have any classes together, our lunches are at different times, and we don't play the same sports."

Adults can't understand sometimes how much relationships change when you're our age. But when you make a Best Moments List, you might be surprised what friend you end up putting on it. If you wrote down the name of someone who used to be important to you, guess what? You can reach back out to that person. A Best Moments List can be a reminder of things and even people you forget you like.

If, on the other hand, you feel like you don't have enough relationships on your list, don't worry. Everyone thinks everyone else has more friends. There's not a teenager alive who thinks, "I've got enough friends right now." And in chapter 10, we're going to talk about what it takes to build a few new relationships.

Lesson 3: Stuff matters less than you think.

Do you know why we want the latest shoes, phone, truck, or video game system? It's not because we're immature teenagers with poor impulse control and an obsession with stuff. It's because we're the most marketed-to generation in the history of the world. It's true, no one has seen more targeted ads than we have.

Search for new headphones online and ten minutes later that exact pair you looked at will show up as an ad in your Instagram feed. Open up Safari and it will be there too. Same goes with TikTok and YouTube. That ad will follow you until you eventually give in and buy the item or you search for something new.

Is that a coincidence? Nope. It's data. You look like a piggy bank to a lot of companies, and they'll do anything to get you shopping.

Despite that new reality, despite the billions of dollars companies spend advertising to us every year, I have a prediction:

Stuff was one of the lowest collections of moments on your list.

How do I know? Because no matter your age, no one who has ever filled out a Best Moments List had stuff as their number one category. Even some of the stuff you listed, upon closer inspection, was probably more about the experience or the relationship.

The ticket stubs to your first NFL game aren't just a souvenir. You don't care about those tiny pieces of paper. There's nothing special about how they were printed. What's special is that your grandfather took you to the game. It's probably more of a relationship moment than it is a stuff moment.

When Ryan Queen graduated from high school, a neighbor gave him a pair of Nike CrossFit shoes. Instead of giving him a tie, a book of motivational quotes, or some item he'd need in a college dorm room, the neighbor honored Ryan's passion for working out. Ryan's dad isn't in his life, so that simple gesture meant even more to him. Those shoes were much more than just an object to Ryan.

Stuff can be fantastic. There's stuff on my list and on McRae's list too. This is by no means an anti-stuff argument, but just be careful that you don't spend your life chasing stuff if it didn't make your list that often.

Lesson 4: Something is missing.

One of the most powerful lessons in this exercise isn't what's on the list but what's missing from it. If you spend a few minutes building a Best Moments List, you might be surprised at what you leave off.

Maybe volleyball was all you cared about in middle school. You spent weekends at tournaments, practiced six days a week, and defined your entire life by the sport. Every birthday present you got was volleyball-related, your mom's car was covered with team stickers, and you always had a volleyball in your hand at home. Now you're a junior in high school, you quit two of the three teams you were on, and it feels like your volleyball obsession is drawing to a natural conclusion.

Did you forget to write it down even once on your list? Don't feel bad. As teenagers, the only thing that changes more often than our relationships is our interests. *Adolescence* is Latin for "experiment." Not really, but it should be. We're going to try a dozen different things, experimenting with hobbies, sports, jobs, and majors to see what fits us best.

McRae did jump rope club. She was in five musicals in middle school and zero in high school. She played lacrosse, ran track and cross-country, and had works of art in multiple shows. And she's exactly where she should be at our age . . . all over the place. The world sometimes puts pressure on us to specialize quickly. At age six we're supposed to pick a sport that we'll play forever. We're supposed to know if we're a theater kid after one play or a coder after one programming class. But take your time. You don't have to be any one thing right now.

But if there's something missing on your list that you thought would at least make a cameo, pay attention to that. The absence might be trying to tell you something.

What did you learn about yourself from your Best Moments List? Maybe it was all four of those lessons. Maybe it was only two. Everybody's experience is a little different, but after you're done looking at it, you'll say the same five words everyone always says:

"I want more of that!"

When you can clearly see what you care about the most, it's only natural to want more of it. You don't have to guess at what makes you happy—you have a list. It's like a grocery list for the life you want to build.

You don't have to stumble around in the dark anymore. The next part of your path is lit, and it's going to lead you one of three places.

TAKE YOUR TIME.

You don't have to be any one thing right now.

JON ACUFF

#HowTeensWin

The Three Performance Zones

Do you remember the story of the tortoise and the hare? That feels a bit too fancy to me. I'm talking about the turtle and the rabbit. No one our age says, "Dear me, is that a hare on the back lawn?" I remember hearing that story when I was a little kid, so if it's been a while since you last heard it, here's a quick summary.

One afternoon, a rabbit is making fun of a turtle because he's so slow. The turtle gets mad and challenges the rabbit to a race. At the start, the rabbit sprints out to a huge lead. He's winning by such a large margin that he decides to show off and take a nap during the middle of the race. While he's asleep by the side of the road, the turtle passes him.

The rabbit wakes up and in a panic tries to catch up to the turtle. Despite a mad gallop at the end, the rabbit loses the race. The moral of the story is "Slow and steady wins the race." It's a tale about the value of consistent effort, but it's also the kind of passage that would make a good SAT question because there's a deeper meaning hidden inside.

The real reason the rabbit lost is because he didn't know about the Potential Zone. You can't blame the rabbit, though, because most people don't know about it either. But we're not most people. Most people don't read this far into a book. Most people don't make a Best Moments List. But you have because you're a high performer.

How do I know that? Because low performers don't read books like this. They don't even know this section of the bookstore exists. But here you are, already on chapter 7. Way to go, you high performer you. But before we celebrate too loudly, I have to warn you. Being a high performer doesn't automatically make you a high achiever.

We've all known people who are capable of occasional bursts of high achievement who couldn't turn it into anything. Why? Because people tend to bounce back and forth between the two most common performance zones:

1. The Comfort Zone
2. The Chaos Zone

The Comfort Zone is when you are stuck. It feels like quicksand. You've got zero actions, zero goals, and zero results. You might be there because you're afraid to try. Maybe you don't know what you want to do with your life, or maybe no one ever told you that you're capable of amazing things. Regardless of the reason, maybe you feel a bit like the rabbit in the middle of the race, taking a nap while the world passes you by.

The Chaos Zone is just the opposite. You've got too many actions, too many goals, and zero results. Have you ever tried to take six AP classes, letter in every sport, hold down an after-school job, and be active with all your friends? Did you feel stressed-out just reading that last sentence? Yeah, me too.

The Chaos Zone is stress city. There are more teens living in this zone than ever before because sports and college prep start so early for us. When my dad played soccer as a kid, travel soccer didn't even exist. You played in the spring, had fun with your friends, and then it was over until next year. Now, most sports are year-round and you have to specialize in one by the time you're three years old. That's a lot of pressure.

The Chaos Zone can also look like perfectionism. Maybe your room was so messy that instead of just cleaning it for a few minutes, you kicked into perfect mode and labeled everything in your drawers. I (McRae) did that once. That wasn't a random example of a situation that could happen, that's what happened. I felt overwhelmed that my whole room was a wreck, so I spent the next two hours organizing the contents of drawers that didn't really matter.

I was sprinting like the rabbit at the end of the race. I was trying to catch up, but I was really going nowhere. That was the real problem with the rabbit. He didn't lose the race because he was slower than the turtle. He lost because he only had two speeds— sprint or sleep. He was running or he was napping, and there was no in-between. He had no middle gear, which is sad because the middle is where the real magic happens. The middle is the Potential Zone.

Think of it like the Goldilocks Zone. It's right between the Comfort Zone and the Chaos Zone. It's not too big, not too small, not too hot, not too cold. It's just right. Right actions, right goals, and right results.

You don't wait around in the Comfort Zone, doing nothing, allowing your room to get steadily more disastrous over the month. You don't run

In the middle is where the real magic happens.

around out of control in the Chaos Zone, deciding to organize every article of clothing you've owned for the last nine years.

You don't skip your homework for most of the semester and then have to score 100 on the final to save your grade. You don't float through the first three years of high school and then try to cram a million extracurricular activities into your life for your college application senior year.

You make steady, easy progress on your goals step by step. You make your bed most days. You put laundry away most days. You empty your backpack most days. Until eventually you notice you're winning a lot of races. You're adding more best moments to your list. You suddenly realize you're changing your life.

If visiting and staying in the Potential Zone sounds impossible, don't worry, it's not. It doesn't even take a lot to change your life. You only have to choose between two options.

Crisis or Tricks

Do you know what one of the best things is about being a teenager?

My dad would probably say, "You don't have to pay for a new hot water heater," but that's only because ours recently died. I suppose it is nice not having to deal with things like roof repairs, the crawl space, taxes, or health insurance, but that's not the best part of being our age.

The best part is that we don't have to look very hard to find our inner child. Our parents, on the other hand, have to go on long mental expeditions to get back in touch with who they were when they were kids. Adults talk about that kind of thing ALL the time. They want to rediscover a sense of childhood wonder and innocence. They'd like to revisit their glory days so they can remember who they wanted to be.

We don't have to do that because we're that age right now. We're already there. We don't need to reflect on days gone by. We're in those days. We don't need to try to imagine what it's like to change, because we're changing constantly. And we're in the perfect place to change the best way—with a voluntary trick.

Two Types of Change

Have your parents ever tried to convince you to stop or start a certain behavior? Maybe they were tired of your being late to school. Maybe there was a class you were failing. Maybe it was how much you use your phone or how long you play video games or what time you go to bed.

It's easy for all of us to think about some part of life that our parents wanted us to improve. My parents are constantly asking me (McRae) to go outside more often. "You need fresh air! A walk around the neighborhood will give you some stress-reducing endorphins. The vitamin D from the sun will make you feel better!" they exclaim from the kitchen on days I hole up in my room.

Do you know why I push back? Do you know why

you have a hard time in those moments too? Do you know why this all-too-common scenario leads to frustration for both you and your parents? Do you know why this type of change feels impossible?

Because no one changes "just because." Child, teen, adult, grandparent—no one wakes up one day and just decides, "I think I'll change my life!" No one rolls out of bed on a random Tuesday and declares, "This is the moment I'll have discipline and grit. I will get to school on time for no other reason than I've had enough of this tomfoolery and I can finally see the error of my ways!"

I think that's how our parents wish change happened, but unfortunately that's not how it works. That's not to say change is a mystery. It's not. It's actually very simple. There are only two reasons people change:

1. Involuntary crisis
2. Voluntary trick

An involuntary crisis is when something outside of your control forces you to change. You get fired from your part-time job and wake up to the reality of how important it is to get to work on time.

You fail a class and have to attend summer school.

NO ONE CHANGES "JUST BECAUSE."

JON ACUFF

#HowTeensWin

On a hot July day, while your friends are at the lake and you're in Chemistry 2, you declare, "THIS WILL NEVER HAPPEN AGAIN."

You get kicked out of a friend group because you gossiped and learn a painful, memorable lesson you'll never forget. Your parents might have told you a hundred times not to talk behind someone's back, but it wasn't until you had to eat lunch by yourself for a week that the lesson set in.

The crisis made you change.

There are two main goals for this book. The first is that you get a glimpse into who you are *today* so that you can take deliberate, fun steps to an amazing *tomorrow*. The second goal is that you get a glimpse into who your parents are so that you can see them as an ally in the journey ahead, not an obstacle. That's not to say that your relationship with them will be perfect, and they might be struggling with their own issues, but a little insight into you and your family can go a long way.

Here's an example of that second goal. Did you know that your parents hope you learn as few lessons from crisis as possible? Why do they hope that? Because it hurts them to watch you hurt.

I recently overheard a father tell another father that his senior son had missed out on some college scholarships because he didn't check his email in time. He lost out on $40,000 because he didn't turn in his application by the correct date.

The college emailed him. His guidance counselor emailed him. But the information he needed sat unread in his unopened inbox. That was an expensive mistake. His father then said something that I think a lot of our parents say when we're not around: "I hope that experience was enough for him to learn that lesson."

What he meant was, "I hope the pain of $40,000 was enough that going forward he'll always check his email. I hope he doesn't have to get fired from a job when he's 27 because he didn't respond to an important client, or lose an opportunity to buy a house at 34 because he didn't open the counteroffer email from his real estate agent."

Let's not beat ourselves up. When you're 15 years old, it's impossible to fully understand that learning how to be responsive with email is a lesson you'll need in your 20s, 30s, 40s, and beyond. No one, including our parents, goes through life with a 20-year lens of how today's actions will impact the next decade's outcomes. But our parents have been to the future we're headed to. They know what's coming, so when they're frustrated at some ball we've dropped, it's often because they want us to arrive to adulthood with as much wisdom and as few bruises as possible.

But sometimes the crisis is what teaches us.

An expensive speeding ticket can often encourage you to change how you drive far better than any lecture could. That's an involuntary crisis and it can educate you. But I, your parents, and even you would rather you didn't need a third-degree burn to know the stove is hot. That brings us to the second way people escape the Comfort Zone—the voluntary trick.

Tricks Are for Kids (and Change)

With a voluntary trick, you change not out of pain but out of joy. (Doesn't that already sound better than that first way?) You simply get such a clear picture of something you want that you realize changing in order to get it is worth it. You recognize something in your life is missing and the reward of what you'll get is worth the work you'll put in to earn it.

You visit a college campus and decide you really want to be on that quad next fall. In order to leave your small town, in order to grasp that sense of freedom of being on your own at your dream school, you have to figure out how to make it happen. You don't faithfully check your email and apply to the scholarships on time "just because it's the responsible thing to do as a mature teenager." You check your email because it's the doorway to the thing you want the most.

No one wants to leave their Comfort Zone. Why would you? It's comfortable! You know the rules and you know what to do. It's familiar and offers the illusion of safety. It's where most adults spend most of their lives.

You know that grumpy adult we mentioned earlier who told you, "Never grow up because it's a trap"? That's a person stuck in the Comfort Zone. They've given up. They've lost touch with their desire. Or worse, they've been numbed to the point of just not caring. You can't blame them. The world does a pretty good job of numbing you.

Binge-watching YouTube numbs you.

Alcohol numbs you.

Social media numbs you.

Vaping numbs you.

Compulsively playing video games numbs you.

If you ever feel disconnected from what you really care about, don't feel ashamed about that. The world is not built for on-fire teenagers. The world is not designed for teenagers who resist the status quo. The world is not built for teenagers who refuse to be average adults with dead-end jobs and quiet lives.

But you can change that. You don't need to wait for a crisis either. We don't need disappointment to wake us up. We don't need a heartbreak to make our hearts beat. We can lean in to desire. We can seize the day. We can rescue ourselves with a voluntary trick, and it all starts with something you're already an expert at—a game.

The Games We Play

It's 3:30 a.m. and I (L.E.) am not tired. I don't usually stay up this late, but this is not a normal night. This is a night we've been working toward for 12 years. This is a night I've been dreaming about for a long time. This is a night that everyone in the entire school talks about.

This is Project Graduation.

A few years ago, parents and teachers realized that graduation night was a dangerous moment for us seniors. Teen traffic accidents tend to increase from April to July—or prom to Fourth of July—every year, and graduation falls right in the middle of that season. They couldn't wait for an involuntary crisis like a car crash to shock the student body into better behavior, so they came up with the best voluntary trick of all—a game.

Project Graduation is an all-nighter held at the school right after the graduation ceremony. From 10 p.m. to 5 a.m., all my friends and I ran around inside the school having fun. There was human foosball in the gym. There was a mechanical bull-riding station. There was king of the hill on a giant inflatable castle. There was cornhole in the halls, Twister in the cafeteria, photo booths in the atrium, and snacks everywhere. Imagine if Willy Wonka's Chocolate Factory got married to a Chuck E. Cheese and then add a healthy dose of glitter just because.

The night culminated with a big prize giveaway in the auditorium. People won laptops, trips, gift cards, and cash. As the sun came up the next morning, students walked out happy, tired, and safe. The night was a huge success, but why did it work?

Because games work. And you've been playing them for years. In fact, you learned how to play games before you could even walk. Peekaboo was your first. Hide-and-seek came next. Tag was probably the third. Teachers used games to teach us how to read in elementary school. Coaches used them to inspire us in middle school. And in high school, games like Project Graduation kept us alive.

Now we're going to use the power of games to

build the lives we want. The great news is they aren't that complicated. There are only five games we have to choose from. Even Chipotle's simple menu is more complicated than that.

Every goal, dream, wish, or hope you have in life will fit neatly into one of five games:

1. School
2. Money
3. Relationships
4. Health
5. Fun

If you want to spend more time in your Potential Zone, being the person you always knew you could be, you just have to answer this first question:

What big game do I want to play?

Here's how they break down.

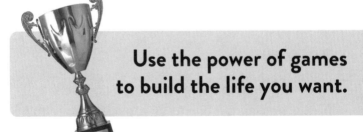

Use the power of games to build the life you want.

School

If you enter the workforce immediately after college or high school, the name of this game changes to "career," but for now it's focused on our education. Want to pass Algebra 2? Want to graduate from high school with an honors diploma? Want to get a partial or even full scholarship to college? Want to be the secretary of the student council? Want to go to cosmetology school and become a hairdresser? Play a school game.

Money

Want to save up to buy a car? Want to pay for that cosmetology school we just talked about? Tired of having an old iPhone that looks like it spent the weekend in the blender? Want to figure out Bitcoin? Want to be that 16-year-old example of the power of compound interest who starts saving when they're a teenager and is a millionaire by the age of 34? Play a money game.

Relationships

Tired of feeling so lonely? Wish you had more friends or even just one really good one? Want to ask somebody out on a date? Need to repair a broken friendship or maybe even end one? Want to plan a fishing trip with a few of the guys in your neighborhood? Wish you had somebody a little bit wiser and a little bit older to talk to about your life? Play a relationship game.

Health

Want to get in better shape? Need to start training for softball season? Ready to drop some bad habit that nobody knows about? Want a better skincare routine because you're tired of acne? Want to improve your mental health? Want to do a better job managing your anxiety? Need to bulk up a little for football or wrestling season? Play a health game.

Fun

This is the final catch-all game. Anything that doesn't easily fit into the first four games lands here. When I made that Rainbow Loom skirt, that was a fun game. When McRae reread all the Harry Potter books, that was a fun game. Want to learn how to knit? Want to figure out how to edit YouTube videos? Want to become a photographer? Want to try out for a play? Determined to make the debate team next year? Play a fun game.

The great thing about this approach is that there's no pressure. It's not an assignment or a test or an obligation. It won't ever be judged or graded. It's just you looking at your life and asking, "What do I want?" You don't even have to start from scratch either. The Best Moments List gives you a huge head start. You've already got dozens of clues about what you really care about. Just ask that question, "What game do I want to play?"

The first time (and maybe even the hundredth time) you ask it, your answer might be "I don't know." But eventually something will stir inside you. It may be quiet initially, especially if you've had a hard time lately—or, you know, if a global pandemic shut down your entire existence for years. But eventually, if you listen to that voice and just pick one of the games to explore, you'll find yourself ready for the second question.

What Do I Win If I Play?

Want to know a secret?

Do you want to know the four words your parents hope they never have to say to you? It's not "You got a tattoo?" or "You bought a snake?" or even "My car is *where*?" Although, let's be honest, they probably don't want to say any of those words either.

There are four very specific words no parent wants to say to you in the middle of an argument:

"Because I said so."

Variations of this regrettable phrase include:

"Because I'm the parent."

"Because I'm your mom."

"Because I'm your dad."

And who can forget the classic "You're under my roof!"

All these words are dreaded by parents because it means they've run out of every other option. It means they've exhausted every other bit of logic and reason in an argument with you. Now they feel backed against a wall and there's no other choice but to blurt out one last Hail Mary: "You have to do that because I said so!"

The "that" can be anything. Maybe they want you to apply yourself to school more. Maybe they want you to finally get your driver's license and relieve the burden of endless carpooling. Maybe they want you to put your shoes on BEFORE you come to the car for church. Maybe they want you to break up with the person you're dating. (Spoiler alert: If you're a parent reading this right now, hating who we are dating rarely has the effect on us that you're hoping for. Exhibit A: Romeo and Juliet.)

There can be a million different reasons your mom or dad says "Because I said so," but when they do, we feel pushed into a corner too. It feels like there's only one way we can respond. Can you guess what I'm about to say? Did you say some version of this just last week?

When we hear "Because I said so," it makes us want to respond, "Well, once I'm 18, you can't tell me what to do."

I am

100

PERCENT

of the people
I am 100 percent
in control over.

JON ACUFF

#HowTeensWin

They throw the parent card, we throw the legal adult card, and no one wins. This type of argument never works because you can't force someone to change. That's a soundtrack we say at our house: "I am 100 percent of the people I am 100 percent in control over." That one cuts two ways. It means (1) I am in control of my own decisions and have to take personal responsibility for them, and (2) I can't make someone else change.

My mom can sign me up for swim lessons, but she can't force me to fall in love with the quiet, mathematical, beautifully introverted nature of the sport. My dad can suggest a book series for me to read, but if my heart's not in it, I won't make it 15 pages into the first one. A well-meaning teacher can suggest a major I should pursue in college, but if I don't buy in, it will never stick.

That's one of the biggest challenges we face at our age. We're making a thousand decisions and most of them are for the very first time. It pains me to admit this, but we need some guidance and advice at times. I (McRae) often feel invincible because that comes with the territory when you're 18, but the truth is that I need help with navigating this weird world.

At the same time though—and here's the tension—we can't ignore our own hearts. We have to balance the outside feedback with the inside hope.

It's important that we feel personally connected to our decisions and dreams.

In the first big question about our goals we asked, "What game do I want to play?" Now it's time to take a deeper step into who we are and who we are becoming to ask the second big question:

What do I win if I play?

Win First, Work Later

As L.E. pointed out in chapter 6, I didn't make any money the summer I spent working at camp. The funny thing to me about that experience is that I spent an entire month doing chores my parents have to force me to do at home.

My dad sometimes jokes that he's worried about my eyesight because I can't see the dishwasher. Whenever I put dirty dishes in the sink instead of putting them into the dishwasher, where he's begged me a hundred times to deposit them, he sarcastically points out how close I got. "You're only 17 inches away. Maybe you need LASIK. Look how close the dishwasher is to the sink, they're practically spooning!" It's not just the dishes either.

I don't keep my room very clean, I leave my stuff all over the house, and I don't take out the trash without a few reminders from my mom. And yet, for weeks I spent hours washing dishes for hundreds of campers I didn't even know. I did trash duty with a smile. I cleaned up like I personally owned the camp.

Why?

Because I answered the question "What do I win if I play?" I mean, if you're going to play a game and spend your most valuable resource on it—your time—you should know the answer to that question before you start. That's the whole point of this book—how teens win.

When I picked camp as the game I was going to play that summer, I came up with a list of what I'd win. Here it is:

1. I'd get to return to Black Mountain, North Carolina, which is beautiful in the summer and a lot cooler than Nashville.

2. My friend did the same program and said it was the best summer she ever had. It will be fun to have that experience in common with her.

3. I'll get to live in a cabin with the other girls doing the program. We'll be a team, and I already feel connected to them in the group chat they started.

4. I'll experience something L.E. has never done. When you're the second kid, you're always quietly looking for ways to do your own thing.

5. I'll meet a lot of girls who might end up going to the same college as me. Maybe I'll even find my future college roommate.

6. I'll get to have a drop-off day. It's exciting to have all your stuff packed into a trunk and see your parents drive away for a month.

7. That said, I'll also get to experience pick-up day. I love walking my parents around the camp and showing them what I've been doing all month.

8. I'll get to serve a lot of other people. This might seem silly, but helping others is one of my favorite things to do.

9. I'll have fun telling people about it when I get home because leaving for a month when you're 17 is a brave thing to do.

10. I'll get a boatload of memories that will carry me through senior year whenever I feel stressed-out.

I didn't sit down and write all of those in a fancy journal one afternoon. I don't want you to feel pressure to do "extra homework" with each exercise in this book. That list existed in two places primarily: my personal thoughts before camp and conversations with my parents.

Those are 10 things I knew I'd win if I worked at the summer camp. Why do they matter? Because the more you win, the more you'll play the game.

I didn't want to read the book they assigned us before camp started. I didn't want to figure out how to pack the right clothes for an entire month. That level of detail makes me feel a little overwhelmed. I didn't really want to empty garbage cans. No teenager ever says, "Yay, hot trash juice!"

In any goal, adventure, or dream, there will be parts you don't want to do, but if what you win is bigger than the work, you'll do it.

"Because I said so" won't get you out of bed on time for school. "Because my parents want me to" might not motivate you most days. "Because it's the

In any goal, adventure, or dream, there will be parts you don't want to do, but if what you win is bigger than the work, you'll do it.

right thing to do" won't always inspire you. Wins, on the other hand—wins you own, wins you come up with—will.

The Power of a Potential Win

You'll do any amount of work if the win is worth it. The classmate who decided to be a songwriter in the eighth grade? They had a win in mind. The friend who found football late in life but then went all in and got to play at Texas A&M? He knew his win. The neighbor who spent months building an art project for a show in a local museum? She had a win all picked out.

You'll do anything if the win is worth it. If Joe Wilson's mom told him to work out before school each day, he would have laughed at her. If his mom tried to wake him up at 5:15 a.m. to hit the gym, he would have rolled over and gone back to sleep. If she tried to force him to spend his weekends doing two-hour weight room sessions, he would have angrily rejected her suggestions. So why does he do all of those things and so many more on his own right now?

Because he owns the win.

Through a bit of trial and error, Joe discovered that he loves the way he feels when he pulls into the parking lot at school after he's worked out that morning. He can literally feel the difference. He also discovered that he likes having a little bit of community with Luke and Ryan, his two workout buddies. It's like they've got a secret club no one else knows about. He likes the muscle he's gaining and the confidence he's building. He likes a dozen little wins, and collectively they make getting up early worth it.

His example holds an interesting lesson for finding a win you care about. What's something you do that if your parents MADE you do it, you wouldn't?

My friend Ben releases silly rap songs that he and his friends record. If his parents made him make music, he would fight against that like every teenager fights against forced piano lessons. My friend Alyssa campaigned for weeks for student council. (Write this down: passing out free snacks, that's the trick to student government.) If her parents made her run for office to pad her college résumé, she wouldn't.

They all do what they do for the win. You should, too, because it's the best way to tap into your full potential.

So, why don't most people do this?

Because dreaming about the win feels a little backward at first. Most of the time, when we begin a new goal, we start with the work we'll have to do, not the reward we'll get. Think about any project you were assigned in class. Were you given a list of rewards or a list of requirements?

Did your teacher say, "When you write this paper with excellence, you'll get the satisfaction of finishing something significant, 10 extra points that will boost your grade, a sneak peek at a writing process you'll desperately need in college and your career, public recognition in class, and—if your parents are the kind of folks who reward good grades—maybe even some cash"? Or did your teacher say, "You need to have three sources, five double-spaced pages, a peer review before you turn it in, and accurate MLA style"?

If you're at the start of a mountain climb and the first thing you come up with is a massive list of all the work you'll have to do to achieve it, do you feel encouraged or discouraged? Which would motivate you more: dreaming about the view from the top and the memories you'll make or thinking about the grueling effort it will take? If you stare at the work, you'll lose sight of the win and never even take the first step. Let's make sure you and I do the opposite of that.

First dream about the win and then decide about the work.

To get started on your wins, just think about a few simple questions.

If you stare at the work, you'll lose sight of the win and never even take the first step.

How to Find a Win

Inside this book, you'll find several exercises that expand the ideas we're covering. Let me say something that's very important: *none of them are mandatory.* That you're reading this book is amazing enough. We added real examples like my list of camp wins and clear steps to create your own wins so that if you want to put this lesson into practice immediately, you can. That said, here are three questions that will help you dig a little deeper into your win list.

Question 1: How will I feel when I accomplish this goal?

I felt special going to camp and doing an adventure my older sister hadn't done. I felt proud when I told my friends about it after it was over. I felt brave watching my parents drive away after dropping me off.

What will you feel if you finish this goal? Feelings

aren't the only thing we'll check in with as we build a win list, but they're a good place to start. If you'd rather do a fill-in-the-blank approach, try something like this:

> When I make the football team, I will feel _____.
> When I get a B in AP US History, I will feel _____.
> When I save up for my own car, I will feel _____.
> When I get the email announcing that I've been accepted to college, I will feel _____.

Question 2: What will I receive when I accomplish this goal?

Sometimes the answer is easy—money! When you get a job making burritos at Moe's Southwest Grill, you get a paycheck. That's how that works. But you also get a sense of purpose. You don't start off on burritos though. Have you ever tried to fold one of those when someone has gone down the entire line and added 67 items to it? Impossible. You gotta earn your way up the Mexican food ladder. (There's always a ladder!) If that seems silly to you, that just means you've never started as the "mop the floors guy" and moved your way up to "burrito guy."

Doing your best at a job can give you a real sense of satisfaction. If you make the high school volleyball team, you get a varsity letter, but you also get a seat at the volleyball table during lunch. If your grades are good enough to join National Honor Society, you get a cord for your gown at graduation. From internal feelings to external rewards, you always get something when you accomplish a goal.

Imagine it's a week, month, or even year from now and you've just crossed the finish line of a new goal—what will you receive?

Question 3: What will I miss if I don't do this?

Let's flip the win question upside down and look at it from another angle. I knew that if I didn't apply to work at camp that summer, I'd lose the opportunity forever. That might sound dramatic, but it's true. The summer after junior year is what the leadership program is designed for. If you want to go the summer after your senior year, you have to be a junior counselor. That's a completely different leadership program that I didn't want to do. I had one shot at one summer program.

How about you? What will you miss if you don't chase your goal?

If you don't apply to that college, you'll never know if you could have gotten in. If you don't write your book now, you won't get to say, "I wrote a book in high school." If you don't ask that person to prom, you might not get to go.

Don't dwell too much on what you'll miss. We're not trying to bring ourselves down with imaginary regret that we sit in all day. What we're doing instead is hacking a life principle that says, "You don't know what you've got until it's gone." Let's not wait until it's gone and we miss it. Let's imagine it's gone, decide if we really want it, and then go get it!

What will you miss if you don't do this?

Once you've got a few wins in place and you feel motivated for what's ahead, it's time to ask the third big question:

How do I win?

Escape the Comfort Zone with an Easy Goal

When my dad was a freshman, he was failing biology. (Please see the introduction of this book where he admits he didn't peak in high school.) His teacher said he could earn some bonus points if he did an extra assignment.

When I (L.E.) bombed a precalculus test in high school, my teachers let me earn extra credit by doing additional problems so that I could bring my grade up to a 70. That's not exactly the bonus points my dad's teacher offered him. All he had to do to earn extra credit was find a dead animal on the side of the road, have flesh-eating bugs strip all the fur, skin, and muscle away, and then rebuild the skeleton.

I don't even know where to begin with this wild story. Maybe this kind of thing happened all the time in the 1990s.

Let's start with the collection of the dead animal from the side of the road. My dad said wherever he went for the next month, he hung his head out the car window and scanned the roadways, hoping to see some poor squirrel that had zigged its last zag. Gross.

Second, where do you find flesh-eating bugs? I bet I could buy some today on Amazon, but remember, my dad grew up in an age called "before the internet." He couldn't just google "flesh-eating bugs" because Google didn't exist.

Third, how do you rebuild a skeleton? My dad was 14, and I know this is going to surprise you, but he was terrible at taxidermy. That didn't faze him though. He's so optimistic about what he's capable of that he thought, "I bet I can just figure this out with a magnifying glass and some glue."

So one afternoon while coming back from the grocery store with my grandmother, he spotted a furry shape in the road. "Stop the car!" he shouted, as he quickly jumped out to retrieve the extra credit critter.

It was so squished that he couldn't tell exactly what it was. Squirrel, muskrat, adolescent groundhog—it could have been anything. He put it in a Tupperware container in the backyard when he got home, hoping that word would spread among the flesh-eating bug community that there was now a free buffet to be had at the Acuff house.

If all went according to plan, in a matter of weeks he'd have a perfectly cleaned skeleton and a passing grade in biology. Instead, it rained that week. A lot. His roadkill Tupperware container turned into the world's worst stew, and eventually he had to admit mushy defeat.

Despite his considerable enthusiasm for the task at hand, he was doomed from the start because of one critical mistake: he made the goal too hard.

This isn't just a teenager thing, it's a human thing. We tend to complicate goals at the beginning. That's Chaos Zone behavior—playing difficult, complex games instead of easing into a new goal and building up momentum first.

I don't know why we do this. Maybe consistently doing the small, easy actions that build up over time feels too slow and boring. Maybe we want complicated solutions because then we don't have to do them. But in my dad's case, it's hard to ignore the fact that he did things the hardest, least productive way ever. And he didn't have to.

Which would have been easier—study a little

more and bring up his grade naturally with better exams and homework that was turned in on time, or find, decompose, and reconstruct a muskrat? (Weirdest sentence in this book.)

He took the hard way out and bombed biology, but we won't. We're going to ask the third big question, "How do I win?" And then we're going to build an Easy Goal.

When It's Worth It

How do I win? If the new best moment is worth it, then naturally this is the next question you ask when it comes to playing a new game. Just imagine . . . you picked a game, you described what you'd win, and now you're thinking, "Ohhh, that win sounds good. I like good things. How do I get that good thing?" Now it's time for some fantastic news: *you win by making the game easy.*

Does that feel a little wrong to you? Maybe you had a coach who preached the power of buckling down, discipline, and willpower. No pain, no gain! Grit, persistence, hustle—those are all great traits, and I hope you continue to develop them as you become an adult, but they won't help you escape the Comfort Zone.

The best way to launch a new adventure is with

YOU WIN
BY MAKING
THE GAME
EASY.

JON ACUFF

#HowTeensWin

an Easy Goal. Adults never tell you that, though, because they're usually too busy making things difficult for themselves. When my dad wrote the book *Finish*, he hired Dr. Mike Peasley to help conduct some research. Together, they studied nearly 900 people for six months as they worked on their goals.

Midway through the project, they realized that most participants overestimated what they could accomplish and unconsciously created impossible games. Instead of stacking the deck in their favor, they came up with wildly difficult goals at the outset and then almost immediately ran into the frustrating constraints of reality.

In other words, their eyes were bigger than their stomach.

Have your parents ever said that to you at a restaurant when you over-ordered a meal? You promised you could eat that entire Western Roundup Breakfast Sampler, but more than a hundred bites in, it looked like you hadn't even made a dent in that tower of flapjacks and you had to throw in the towel. That's what happens to people with their goals.

To address that common problem, my dad encouraged his research participants to cut their goals in half. What happened next was surprising. People who took this unusual approach were 63 percent more successful. The people who made the games easier won more often.

Why did this happen?

Because regardless of whether you're 15 or 55, we all have access to the same exact goal ladder. If you climb it the right way, you consistently build a life bursting at the seams with best moments. If you climb it the wrong way, you become one of the 92 percent of people who, according to researchers at the University of Scranton, never finish their New Year's resolutions.[1]

What's the right way, the best way, and really the only way to climb a ladder? From the bottom up.

Here's how it works:

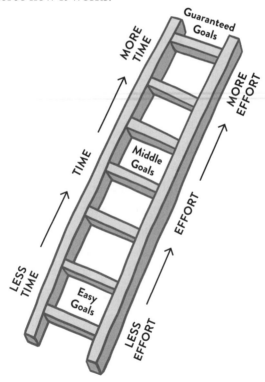

A ladder, no matter how big it is, has two parts: vertical rails and horizontal rungs. In the goal ladder, one vertical rail is effort and the other vertical rail is time. At the bottom of the ladder, you don't have to use a lot of time or effort to achieve your goals. Easy Goals are simple to reach and you barely have to take your foot off the ground. Reading five pages of a history book, walking half a mile in your neighborhood, making your bed twice this week—no one would say, "Ugh, it took me forever to accomplish those goals and the effort was unbelievable!"

The higher you climb the ladder, from Easy Goals to Middle Goals and eventually to Guaranteed Goals, the more time and effort it takes you.

People often want to start with Guaranteed Goals because they're the most ambitious. "Go big or go home!" is a good mantra for a football locker room, but that attitude has also sent thousands of students back to the Comfort Zone when unmet, unrealistic expectations crush them. They essentially fall off the goal ladder and give up.

Imagine right now you're standing at the bottom of a 12-foot ladder. You know the one I mean. It's the ladder your dad yells for you to hold while he cleans the gutters of your house. You get on your phone for 30 seconds and he acts like you've left him clinging to the side of Mount Everest. If I told you that your goal is to get to the top of that ladder, you would have two options:

1. Climb up it step by step, starting from the bottom.
2. Jump as high as you can and try to grab the top rung.

Before you make your decision on which option is best, let me remind you that it's a 12-foot ladder. That means the top rung is two feet higher than an NBA rim. Have you ever dunked before? That's only 10 feet. Have you ever touched the top of a basketball backboard? Me either. But I have climbed to the top of a ladder. It wasn't even that hard. And it always starts with the first rung, which is an Easy Goal.

How do you build one? With five key conditions.

The Ladder Starts Here

Have you ever taken an open-book exam? They're the best because all the answers are right there! That's what we're about to do with our Easy Goals. You don't have to guess how to create one. Just take a game you want to play (school, money, relationships, health, or fun) and then look for these five conditions.

1. Easy Goals have short time frames.

An Easy Goal can be accomplished in one to seven days. If it takes you a month to finish, it's not an Easy Goal. For example, when I (McRae) was a freshman, I knew the lacrosse team had a one-mile time trial. I wanted to be in the top three for my grade, but that was a big goal. That took me months to work on. An

Easy Goal, which is essentially a smaller version of a massive goal, would be "run twice this week." That's a goal I could work on right away and finish in a short time frame.

Want to become a famous YouTuber? That's a massive goal. Want to sign up for a YouTube channel and post your first video? That's an Easy Goal you can do this week.

Want to save up to buy your first car? That's a massive goal. Want to apply to work at the local grocery store that you can walk to from home? That's an Easy Goal you can do tomorrow.

2. Easy Goals have obvious first steps.

If there's even the slightest confusion at the start of your goal, your stuck self—that part of you that doesn't want to change—will shout, "Never mind!" and give up. With an Easy Goal, you can always figure out what to do next. Here are a few examples of good first steps for each of the five games.

School

- Ask one teacher for help on one assignment.
- Read the academic requirements for a college you're interested in. (Applying, getting letters of recommendation, and writing essays are bigger

Middle Goals, but reading the requirements is easy.)

- Spend 15 minutes today on an essay that's due next week.

Money

- Think of three ways you could make a little money this summer.
- Have your parents take you to the nearest used bookstore and sell a few of the books you've already read (or clothes at a vintage store).
- Find one thing you want to save up for and make it the wallpaper on your phone.

Relationships

- Text a friend an encouraging message.
- Invite a friend you haven't seen for a while over to your house to make brownies or connect online to play your favorite video game.
- Thank your parents for doing something small, like driving you to school.

Health

- Do 20 jumping jacks in your room.
- Spend 10 minutes outside.
- Journal about how today felt.

Fun

- Make a list of your top 10 favorite songs and listen to a few.
- Finish a paint-by-numbers set or a puzzle.
- Make a Shutterfly photo book of your best moments from last summer.

Those 15 examples will help you get started on your first step, and once you do, you'll be surprised at how easy it is to find the next one. That's how you build momentum. You take the first step, push through any fear and doubt, and then find out that the second step was hidden right behind it. Guess where the third step is hiding? Right behind the second one. Before you know it, you're on a roll, leaping from step to step to step like a rock skipping over water.

3. Easy Goals are not expensive.

I once saw some girls playing cornhole with their phones. Instead of throwing bean bags, they were throwing iPhones. They knew that if they broke them, their parents would buy them the newest version. That is not the type of parents I have.

If you're not currently sitting on a pile of cash,

don't worry, me either. The good news is that an Easy Goal doesn't require much (if any) money. Let's say you want to join the mountain bike club at your school. What's an easy first step? See if you can borrow someone's bike and go on a few rides in your neighborhood. If your goal is to start collecting vinyl records, get a $50 record player at Walmart and buy two albums. If you want to gain a few pounds of muscle for baseball season, get a small sample of protein powder first instead of buying that gigantic bag they sell at Costco with 822 servings.

If your initial goal costs a lot of money to accomplish, you've just given your stuck self an amazing excuse not to do it. This inexpensive approach also makes it easier for your parents to support you. If you borrow a bike, ride a dozen times in the neighborhood, and research what bike most of the members of the team ride, you'll have far greater success when you ask your parents if they'll split the cost of a new bike with you. And I'll let you in on a little secret: most parents are thrilled when you find a hobby, class, or sport you love and will do everything they can to help you dive deeper into it. As any mom who has sat in the parking lot for hours each week during dance lessons will tell you, parents will move heaven and earth when you find a passion that inspires you.

4. Easy Goals are fun!

Being a teenager is not easy. Adults often look back on adolescence as if it's the glory days, but that's just because they forget what it's really like. Do you know what my mom never has to worry about? Who she will sit with at lunch today. That's not a tense moment for her. She doesn't have to wonder if someone is going to ask her to prom. She doesn't waste a second thought on where she'll be able to stand at the football game, whether she'll get into college, or if she's going to fail that class. But we are dealing with all those challenges and so many more. So when it comes to adding a new goal to your already busy life, make sure it's got at least a little bit of fun built in.

If your big goal is to get into college, start your Easy Goal with something fun. Watch hype videos from five different college football teams to get a sense of what you could be doing on your Saturdays in the fall. Follow "outfits of the day" Instagram accounts from sororities you could join. Talk to friends who are older than you and ask them about their favorite parts of their school.

If your big goal is to save up for a new car, go to the local Cars and Coffee meetup one weekend to get excited about a dream car you can own when you're an adult. Make a list of the first five places you want to drive when you finally get behind the wheel. Search used car sites to see what might be possible if you work enough hours at an after-school job.

There's plenty of time for the hard work later, but when you're at the bottom of the ladder, a boost of fun can be just what you need to keep climbing.

5. Easy Goals feel like they're not enough.

My friend's mom is a "maximizer." She doesn't plan family vacations, she wins family vacations. When they visited the Grand Canyon, she didn't want to just stand on the edge and take a photo like everyone else. She wanted to experience every inch of it. But from Phoenix you can't drive to the canyon, fly over it in a helicopter, take a boat ride on the Colorado River, and have a picnic at the bottom all on the same day . . . unless you charter a small plane. So that's what she did. No time for driving!

At the crack of dawn, they drove to a local airport and the plane flew them close to the Grand Canyon. They hopped on a bus for a tour of a Native American Reservation. No time for questions! They jumped into a helicopter that flew them to the bottom of the canyon where they immediately got into a boat. No time for photos! They quickly floated down the Colorado River to the picnic spot. No time for chewing!

Car, plane, bus, helicopter, boat—they did all of that in one day. And then they did it all in reverse to get back to their hotel. Did they collapse when they returned? No. No time for collapsing! They showered as fast as they could and went to dinner at a fancy French restaurant to celebrate someone's birthday. No time for cake!

That's an impressive (and exhausting) day. Do you know what's the opposite of that approach? Easy Goals. Easy Goals aren't over-the-top. You don't have to sprint around, constantly out of breath, trying to accomplish something impossible. Easy Goals build small structures. They give you a foundation. They offer you that first bit of momentum. If you feel like you're not doing enough yet, that's a good sign.

Jeffery J. Downs and Jami L. Downs wrote a book about consistency titled *Streaking*. "Streaking" is a term that just means you do an activity every day for a certain number of days. For example, if your baseball team has won five games in a row, you have a five-game win streak. Their book teaches you how to accomplish massive goals in tiny ways. One of their rules is that the Easy Goal you decide to pursue should be so simple it's laughable. When you share it with friends, their response should be "Is that all?" Jami says, "If the activity sounds impressive when said aloud, it is probably too hard."[1]

To build a good Easy Goal, use those five factors like a filter.

If it takes you all semester to accomplish, it's not easy.

If you can't figure out what to do next, make it smaller.

If it forces you to beg your parents for money, find a cheaper way to do it.

If it's boring, figure out how to make it enjoyable.

If friends are amazed when you mention it at lunch, listen to Jami—it's too hard.

Easy Goals make escaping the Comfort Zone . . . easy.

Time Is in Our Favor

How many Easy Goals should you try? As many as you want. Why? Because you're young!

Sometimes I get to go on trips with my dad to speaking events. (He speaks to companies about the books he writes to help their employees accomplish more goals.) After his speech, people will often ask him questions in the hotel lobby. It's always interesting to watch him tailor his advice based on the age of the person he's talking to. If a 52-year-old says they want to radically change careers, my dad will ask specific questions like "What are your monthly expenses?" "How much money do you have saved up?" "Do you have any kids?" and "What kind of debt do you have?"

He's trying to get a sense of the person's responsibilities before he gives them feedback. But if the person asking for advice is 22, not 52, he uses completely different questions. Then he just asks, "What are you waiting for?"

If the 22-year-old chases 100 Easy Goals for a year and none of them work, so what? They'll be 23 years old with a year's worth of valuable experience and won't have abandoned the responsibility of being a parent, spouse, or homeowner, because more than likely they are not any of those things. They're 22! They've got the whole world ahead of them, and so do we.

You should chase your goals until you're 102 years old, but let's be honest—the greatest time in your entire life to try as many Easy Goals as you possibly can is right now. Don't miss it! Climb every hill. Cross every ocean. Shout every song. Turn over every rock. Show the entire world how teens win. And when you find a few goals you love, transform them into Middle Goals.

The greatest time
in your entire life
to try as many **Easy Goals**
as you possibly can is

RIGHT
NOW

JON ACUFF

Middle Goals

There's a boy in our neighborhood who climbed the goal ladder with a lawn mower.

That's a strange visual, but allow me (L.E.) to explain. About six summers ago, I noticed a high school student pull up to our neighbor's yard with the handle of a lawn mower sticking out the back window of an old Toyota 4Runner. A skinny teenager got out, surveyed the situation, and then began making neat lines across the lawn. His car was a little beat-up, the lawn mower was a little beat-up, even the hat he wore to shade himself from the hot Tennessee sun was a little beat-up, but he didn't seem to mind. He mowed his way through the entire summer, yard by yard, day by day.

I saw him again the next summer, but this time he had a lawn mower, a weed whacker, and an edger. His tool kit was growing. His skills got better, his client list expanded, and now he had a little money to invest in his small business. The third summer he returned with an actual landscaping trailer.

Gone were the days of just trying to cram his gear into the back of his SUV. A massive zero-turn riding mower sat on the trailer. (I had to google that product name—did it sound like I knew what I was talking about?) The simple push mower was gone, and he was moving his way up in the world. (My dad was desperate for me to say "he was *mowing* his way up in the world," but I assured him that was the daddest of all dad jokes.)

The summer after that, even the old 4Runner disappeared. Now he had a pickup truck pulling the trailer. The next summer the pickup truck was wrapped with the name of his business. One lawn, one summer, one beat-up lawn mower had turned into his livelihood. That's how the goal ladder works.

He didn't buy that expensive lawn mower the first summer. He just did a bunch of Easy Goals. He mowed a few yards to see if this would turn into anything. Along the way, I bet he asked himself a few questions:

"Do I enjoy doing this?"

"Do I want to get better at doing this?"

"Do I understand how this game is played?"

"Do I want to take the next step?"

If the answer to those questions had been "no," I doubt I would have seen him a second summer. He would have found another way to fill his time. But in this case, his answer must have been "yes" because he kept taking the next steps up the ladder with a Middle Goal. Again, he didn't buy the truck that second summer. He didn't advertise his business that third summer. He might have burned out if he did.

Have your parents ever gone all in on a new hobby or activity? Maybe they played pickleball one time at a friend's house and then decided to buy carbon fiber paddles, join three leagues, and build a court in your backyard. A year later, they never play and the court is just an odd relic of what happens when you overdo it. That's the Chaos Zone, where you're either all in or all out.

We're going to avoid that like our teenage landscape architect did so perfectly. We're just going to take an Easy Goal we like and turn it into a Middle Goal with five conditions.

1. Middle Goals have a time frame of 30 to 90 days.

Mowing a neighbor's yard one time only takes a day. That's an Easy Goal. Selling that same neighbor a summer package where you promise to mow each week from June to August takes three months. That's a Middle Goal. When McRae worked on her mile time for lacrosse, that was a Middle Goal. It took her eight weeks to get ready. Becoming an Eagle Scout is a great goal, but it's not a Middle Goal. It takes years to accomplish that.

The time it takes to achieve your goal is the clearest sign as to what type of goal it really is. It's also a great clue that maybe you shouldn't turn an Easy Goal into a Middle Goal. If doing an Easy Goal for one to seven days felt like a hassle, listen to yourself and pursue something different.

2. Middle Goals are flexible.

We're using Middle Goals to develop consistency, so it's important that we have a bunch of ways we can work on them. The more actions we have that move us forward, the easier it is to accomplish a goal. For example, let's say you want to pass macroeconomics. It's your least favorite class, it doesn't make any sense to you, and you got the hardest teacher in the school. In order to finish this goal, you'd throw as many actions at it as possible. You could start by making a list that included:

- Take careful notes in class.
- Work with your teacher after school for some additional tutoring.
- Review answers you got wrong on the last test so you won't get them wrong on the next one.
- Ask a friend for help because sometimes a classmate can explain it in a way that makes even more sense.
- Watch YouTube videos on specific concepts that are tripping you up.
- Do practice questions so by the time the real test comes around you feel ready.
- Knock out every opportunity for extra credit that your teacher offers.

When you're in a stressful situation, fear always tells you that there's nothing you can do. Fear loves to say, "You're all out of options." But you can usually come up with a list of actions if you think about the challenge for a few minutes. Why does flexibility with our actions matter? Because if the only action on your list was "work with your teacher after school for some additional tutoring," guess what would happen on the days when your teacher isn't available?

Nothing.

You wouldn't be able to work on your goal. You'd be stuck. But if you're flexible and have 10 different actions you can do, you'd always be able to make a little progress no matter what was happening. Think about it like a Swiss Army knife. Each action is a new tool you're adding to it so that you're forever ready.

3. Middle Goals don't fall apart if you miss a day.

Sometimes adults think our generation is lazy. They worry that we're obsessed with video games and social media but don't care about school. I don't think that's true though. I see the opposite in me and my friends. If anything, we put tremendous pressure on ourselves.

Let's take sports as an example. You can't just play casually anymore. Now you have to pick one sport and specialize when you're a toddler. Cheerleading, for instance, isn't just at football games. There are regional competitions every weekend, massive events at Disney World, and private lessons to make sure you hit your back tuck. There are cuts and consequences at every corner, along with thousands of dollars of expenses for our parents. We all became full-time athletes without even realizing it was happening. The worst part is that if you don't participate in some life-consuming after-school activity, it feels impossible to have friends because they're all off participating in one themselves.

When adults would ask me what I was doing in the summer during high school, I would say, "Band." They didn't understand how that could fill a whole summer because they were imagining the version of adolescence they experienced. Ours is a lot busier.

Don't get me wrong, I think the pace we push ourselves at can be a lot of fun, and I'd rather be busy than bored, but it can often cause bouts of perfectionism. You feel a pressure to do it all perfectly. But with a Middle Goal you don't have to. You're aiming for consistency, not perfection.

You're going to miss a few days. There's a big chance you won't go 30 for 30 or 90 for 90. When you mess up, give yourself permission to try again. If you can learn resilience as a teenager, which is just the ability to begin again when things don't go your way, you'll have a tool that will make being an adult so much easier.

If you can learn resilience as a teenager, you'll have a tool that will make being an adult so much easier.

4. Middle Goals encourage you to tweak your schedule.

You barely have to touch your schedule to accomplish an Easy Goal, but a Middle Goal requires a little more focus. Can you find 3 percent of your week to work on your goal? That's roughly five hours, or 40 minutes a day. I know it may sound like we carry stopwatches at the Acuff house and my parents are constantly barking out orders like "You've got 11.4 minutes to get ready for school and only 3.7 minutes to eat your breakfast!" but I promise that's not the case. What I'm trying to do is use one of the only universal measurements in life—time—to apply some helpful boundaries around otherwise shapeless goals. I don't like school projects with casual instructions because then I don't really know how to finish them. An assignment that says "have some sources for your paper" is less helpful than one that says "have four scholarly sources for your paper."

With a Middle Goal, we're climbing the ladder, which means our effort and our time are going to increase. If I tell you that I'm too busy to turn an Easy Goal into a Middle Goal, what I'm saying is I'm too busy to find 3 percent of my week. What if your mom asked you to clean 3 percent of your room? What would that take—putting away one small pile of laundry or making up half of your bed? You could do that without changing your week much. Middle Goals take more time than Easy Goals, but it's still not much.

5. Middle Goals work best when you ask for help.

I have a very helpful, tall father who, again, is prone to pop into this book and insert his own slightly exaggerated adjectives. But in all seriousness, when you write a book for teenagers, you never want to assume everyone has a perfect home life. I have friends who haven't seen their dad in years. I have friends who lost their mom to cancer. I have friends who feel like strangers in their own families now that their mom is remarried and has started a new one. So when I tell you that a Middle Goal works best when you ask for help, don't hear that it has to be your parents. Your source of help might be your mom or dad, but if it's not, that's okay.

It could be your favorite teacher or coach. It could be your boss or your small group leader from church. It might be a neighbor. My dad has helped a dozen seniors write their college essays because applying to schools is a wonderful Middle Goal. Dean Johnson got into shape his sophomore year by working with a trainer. That "bonus parent" was able to encourage and motivate him in a way that his own dad couldn't. His dad is fantastic. He's super active in Dean's life but also humble enough to realize it does indeed take a village.

You can accomplish Easy Goals all on your own, but a Middle Goal requires a little help. The good news is that adults love to help motivated teenagers. A CEO of a company is more likely to encourage a 15-year-old who is trying to start a business than a 45-year-old. You'll be amazed at how many people actually want to help our generation. It's one of the benefits of being our age. Don't miss it. Ask for help.

What Middle Goals should you try? Well, what Easy Goals did you love?

That's often what happens—you try something, sometimes even on a whim, and discover to your surprise that you really enjoy it. Jennifer Luoto, an eighth grader, tried high jump and found out she had a real knack for it. The pattern of steps as you approach it, the way you arch your back, the need to suspend any fear that you might land on your head—it all just made sense to her. It was a health game she tried just because, and when she did, the results were shocking. She jumped all the way to the state championship.

Jennifer hadn't spent years training for that moment. She did an Easy Goal that turned into a Middle Goal. Will it turn into a Guaranteed Goal someday? Will she carry it into high school and maybe even college? Will the high jump become her focus going forward, the game she plays above all others? Time will tell, but if she does, it will mean that she tapped into what we need to tap into next: the four Potential Zone fuels.

The Four Fuels

I (L.E.) have never run out of gas. I've never even come close because my parents are such cautious people. They didn't teach me to fill up when my fuel light comes on. They didn't even teach me to get more gas when the tank only has a quarter left. Oh no, their "it's time to think about gas" is half a tank. If I get to half a tank, they want me to consider refueling soon. If that seems a bit extreme to you, I agree. That is VERY cautious, but it has made fuel something I think about often.

I am never going to run my car out of gas, but that's not what we're talking about here. There's a different source of energy that really drives us, and when it runs low, most people will stall out in life. Have you ever felt uninspired, like you couldn't move an inch on a project or a goal? That's a fuel issue. Have you ever felt burned out, like you were over it—whatever "it" was? That's a fuel issue. Have you ever seen a friend who is so high-performing and motivated that it makes you wish you were that inspired about your own life too? That's a fuel issue.

Being a teenager is kind of like waking up one day and finding a Ferrari in the woods. We've got this new body, new emotions, new EVERYTHING, and we don't know what to do with it. We know that a Ferrari can go fast. We know it's built for adventures. We know it's designed for the open road, hairpin corners, and cliffside vistas, but it won't move an inch until we find the right fuel.

Take Your Pick

Ferraris only run on one type of fuel, but the Potential Zone is a little different. It will actually accept four types:

1. Impact
2. Joy
3. Community
4. Stories

If you want to accomplish amazing things with your life, all you have to do is use these four fuels. The wins you pick will get you started up the goal ladder, and the right fuel will keep you going.

Fortunately, these fuels will feel a little familiar because they're essentially the greatest versions of the categories you found hidden in your Best Moments List. Do you remember how we broke our lists down? We labeled each moment as win, experience, relationship, or stuff. That was just the beginning of how the Best Moments List will help you build your future, though, because those categories overlap with the four fuels.

Your best win will impact the world.

Your best experience will fill you with joy.

The best relationships always lead to community.

The best stuff tells a story.

Those are the four most powerful, most sustainable fuels for succeeding at your Middle Goals. The truth is, Middle Goals are challenging. If you really want to work on something for 30 to 90 days, you need much more motivation than you had with your Easy Goal. You need a fuel.

How do you know which one might work best for you? Well, if the majority of your best moments were relationship-based, guess which fuel will inspire you the most? Community. If experiences filled your list, can you imagine which of the four will motivate you? Joy. If wins lit you up, so will impact. If stuff was what dominated your list, then stories will encourage you. If you were a mix of all four categories, then get ready for a unique mix of all four fuels. Everyone uses them a little differently.

I'm more about joy. McRae is more about community. Both are great because they get our individual Ferraris moving in the right direction—forward. If you're ready to see what yours can do, let's break down each fuel.

Achieve the Best Kind of Accomplishment

By the time you're reading this book, there will be a new Stanley cup. By that I (McRae) don't mean the championship trophy they give to professional hockey teams. I mean the massive water jug everyone at my school covets.

Do you have one? Is that just a girl thing? I feel like boys drink out of water faucets in the hall or puddles in the parking lot. I don't know where they're getting their liquids from, but we girls are desperate to stay hydrated at all times. Maybe it's just a different version of a sippy cup.

We tend to take water for granted because it's always available, but Scott Harrison doesn't. That was never his plan, to make water his life, but you can't really predict where the fuel of impact will take you. Scott couldn't imagine how impact would change him, especially when he was 28 years old and seemingly had it all.

Scott was a successful club promoter in New York City. He drove a BMW, had a grand piano in his Manhattan apartment, dated models from the covers of fashion magazines, and spent his weekends bouncing from Milan to Paris to London.

His job was simple: pack beautiful clubs with beautiful people who would overpay for drinks. And he was good at it. Companies paid him thousands of dollars a month just to be seen holding their products. He was an influencer before the internet even existed. After a childhood spent taking care of an invalid mother, Scott was living the big city dream, and he had it all—right up until his short-term fuels started to sputter out.[1]

You can accomplish wonderful things with fame, money, and power, but they're better as a consequence for a life well lived instead of as a cause for living your life. In his late 20s, Scott came to a place that most wildly successful people don't reach until much later in life.

"I realized, wow, there would never be enough," he told my dad in a podcast interview. "If I died, there would be no purpose for my life. My tomb-stone would read, 'Here lies a club promoter who got a million people wasted,' full stop." I don't know if they'll even carve such a depressing statement on a tombstone, but Scott knew he wasn't tapping into his full potential—not by a long shot.

"I was emotionally, morally, and spiritually bankrupt," he said. Have you ever felt that low? With the rate of depression as high as it is for teen-agers right now, I think that's a feeling a lot of us can relate to. Scott didn't want to sit in that spot anymore. "I wanted to reinvent my life completely and see if I could find purpose, to see if I could be useful."

Can I be useful? Can I make a difference? Can my life matter? Questions like that are often the front door to one of the best fuels we all have access to: impact. But how do you do that as a club promoter? It's a fairly vain set of skills and not the background you'd imagine a world-changer possessing. If you're reading this right now and thinking, "But what can I do? I'm just a kid," Scott was feeling the same way: "What can I do? I'm just a club promoter."

Scott was stuck, but he did have a degree in photo-journalism that he'd barely acquired. "I was a C−/D+ student," he admitted. Hooray for authentic stories where adults don't pretend they were perfect their entire lives and lecture us teens that we need to do better! With a camera and charisma, Scott talked his way on board a hospital ship headed to Liberia, one of the poorest countries in the world.

He didn't have a perfect plan. He didn't have a 10-year vision. He just knew that the Comfort Zone wasn't working so well anymore, and he was in too much pain to stay the same.

In Liberia, the Mercy Ships ocean liner full of medical personnel set up a hospital in a soccer stadium with 1,500 slots for medical care. As Scott stood there capturing this first experience, he was stunned to see that more than 5,000 people showed up. "We sent 3,500 sick people home with no hope because we didn't have enough doctors and we didn't have enough resources. I remember weeping because I later learned that these people had walked for more than a month from neighboring countries just to see a doctor. They were bringing their kids with them from Sierra Leone, Côte d'Ivoire, and Guinea, just hoping that maybe a doctor could save their child, and we didn't have enough doctors."

It was Scott's first real shock in West Africa, but it wasn't his last. "When I went into the rural areas, I saw people drinking dirty water for the first time in my life. You have to contrast this with the idea that I sold Voss water for $10 [a bottle] in our clubs just weeks before." Remember that Stanley cup? What if you couldn't see through the water inside it because it was so polluted?

As the days rolled on and Scott's humanitarian education continued, a statistic stood out to him that offered a possible solution to all the hardship. "I learned that 50 percent of the disease in the country was caused by unsafe water, a lack of sanitation and hygiene. It was a eureka moment."

He ran back to the ship and talked to the chief medical officer, who had been working in that area for 25 years. "I told him, 'People are drinking water that is killing them,' and he said to me, 'Why don't you go work on that problem? I'm going to help thousands of people every year using my hands through surgery, but you could be the greatest doctor in the world if you just got 700 million people clean water.'"

You can interpret a moment like this one of two ways. It's either an impractical dream with insurmountable odds or an inexhaustible fuel for change. Scott chose the latter.

When you get a glimpse of the impact you can make, the size of a problem becomes your ally because it means your drive to solve it will never quit.

Scott returned to New York City with fresh wind in his sails. He didn't have a detailed plan for his

The size of a problem is your ally because your drive to solve it will never quit.

nonprofit, so he started his mission with what he had.

"The only idea I had was to throw a party in a nightclub for my birthday. I figured I could get a club and an open bar donated for my friends." You usually don't have to become an entirely different person to change the world. You often just have to use the gifts you already have but in slightly different ways.

Scott sent out an email that said, "It's my 31st birthday. Come to the meatpacking district in New York, and make a $20 donation to get in the club." That casual party was the first day of Charity Water, and they ended up raising $15,000 in cash that night.

Fifteen years later, Scott and Charity Water have raised $750 million to bring clean water to almost 17 million people in 29 countries.

That's impact, a fuel that will not run out, and you have the exact same access to it that Scott does.

Finding Your Africa

When you hear amazing stories like Scott's, it's difficult not to immediately think, "I could never do that." Me either. That's actually the same response Scott would've had if you had tried to tell him the middle of the story when he was in the beginning of it. On that day when he was crying in a soccer stadium as he watched parents carrying their sick children home, if you had said, "Don't worry, Scott, you're going to raise $750 million and change the world," he wouldn't have believed you.

He would've said the same thing you might be thinking right now: "I could never do that." He wasn't ready for that reality. All he was ready to do was throw a party in a nightclub and try to see if this thing could be a thing. That's how impact always starts. It's small and it comes in many different forms.

You don't have to raise $750 million to change the world. Sometimes all you have to do is help someone the way someone else helped you.

Jadyn Fenton spends 10 weeks each summer at Hopetown. I know you're probably expecting this will be just like my own camp story, but I promise you this one is different.

She doesn't work there for the money.

She doesn't work there for the prestige.

She doesn't even work there for the community like I did at my camp.

She works there because she gets it.

Hopetown isn't an ordinary summer camp. It was established 27 years ago by Daystar, a counseling center for kids in Nashville. Run by Sissy Goff and David Thomas, Daystar has helped thousands of kids process thousands of challenges. If you're feeling low about school, you can go talk to them. If your parents got divorced and you feel pulled in two different directions, you can go talk to them. If your school experienced a tragedy, you can go talk to them.

Inside a bright, cheery house, you'll find counselors who care, a popcorn machine with as much popcorn as you want, and dogs who are always willing to sit on the couch next to you during your therapy session. You'll also find Jadyn Fenton.

She's gone to Daystar for years. To say she grew up there would be an understatement. From a little girl with recently divorced parents to a strong young woman who helped her single mom wrangle her two rambunctious little brothers, Jadyn has blossomed. Daystar impacted her in ways she can never repay, but she tries.

She volunteers there. She helps out when there

are special circumstances. She speaks at their annual fundraising event. And she spends her summer at Hopetown, their weeklong camp for kids who are figuring out complicated lives. (And what teenager doesn't have a complicated life?)

Jadyn gets it.

She's been impacted, so impact is a fuel that drives her too.

She wants another kid to feel as welcomed as she was that first day.

She wants another student to know they've got a future.

She wants another kid without a mom or a dad to know they're not alone.

Whether impact finds you in Africa like Scott or closer to home like Jadyn, the result is the same: you change the world.

In small ways, in big ways, in a million in-between ways—when you dare to chase a dream, you often impact others in ways you don't even see.

For example, if you go after a "reach school," that has ripples. Other students see you trying. Your siblings see you trying. Even adults in your neighborhood see you trying. You might think you're just trying to accomplish something for yourself—to be the first person in your family to go to college or the first person in your high school to attend

West Point—but that personal goal has community impact.

The bigger your goal, the bigger the dent you leave on the universe. How will you impact the world? I can't wait to see!

Joy Is a Fuel

I (L.E.) didn't bring my lovebird Buddy to college with me.

We're not allowed to have pets in the dorm, but even if we were, I wouldn't have brought Buddy. There are certain pets that get you labeled. If you own a snake, for instance, you're a "snake guy." If you own a turtle, you're a "turtle guy." If you own a bird, you're a "bird girl."

No one ever says that about dogs. If you own a dog, nobody says, "That L.E., can you believe she owns a dog? She's a total dog girl." They don't really even say that about cat ladies unless you own a bunch. One cat? Cool. Eleven cats? Yikes.

I couldn't bring my bird because I was already bringing something else fairly unusual—my piano.

My mom tried to buy me a smaller one for my dorm room. She knew I'd have a hard time fitting it in the room. She knew my roommate might not want to hear me practicing. She knew I'd probably be the only girl on my floor with a full-sized, 88-weighted-keys, electric piano shoved under my bed. I didn't care because it gives me joy.

The fastest way to understand joy as a fuel is that it's an experience you do "just because."

I won't ever become a professional musician.

I didn't get a scholarship to play the piano.

I probably won't even take a single piano class in the four years I'm here.

That doesn't matter, though, because the piano isn't for anyone else—it's for me.

My parents have heard me play five times in the last 10 years. That's right, I took lessons for a decade but never signed up for a recital. I practice when I'm home, but I wear headphones. One afternoon, my mom said, "What if L.E. doesn't know how to play? Maybe she's just banging around up there making stuff up?"

It's a fair question, but my parents know why I'm doing it.

Joy is the fuel that motivates me.

I didn't get paid to weave an entire skirt out of Rainbow Loom bracelets.

No one but me really enjoys the photo wall it took me hours to arrange, update, and maintain.

And the skimboard caught everyone off guard except me.

One summer, we went to Tybee Island, an Atlantic coast beach just outside of Savannah, Georgia. On the first day we were there, my dad bought me a skimboard because I was interested in learning how to do that. I used it so much that first day, it broke in half. We quickly discovered that skimboards are only sold in two varieties:

1. Amateur level, made of cheap plywood and spray-painted with the phrase "Rad Summer!" for $14.
2. Professional level, made of fiberglass and apparently pure unicorn horn for $300.

There is no middle option. I know that because my parents kept saying "There is no middle option!" while we walked around the surf store looking for a new skimboard. My first eight-hour skimboarding session was enough to clue them in that I was not done though. They could tell that I was just getting started.

Was I going to become a professional skimboarder? Nope.

Was I the only one of my friends who skimboards? Yep.

Did I blow through six months of savings to split
the cost of the fancy new version with my parents?
You better believe it.

Did my feet bleed a little bit by the seventh day of
doing nothing but skimboarding? Yes, yes they did.

I found a new joy.

Has that ever happened to you?

Have you ever stumbled onto something you care
so much about that you don't care if anyone else is
into it? Maybe it was a book series or a movie or a
video game. It could even be an app. Your friends
have long given up on *Pokémon GO*, but you're still
catching them all.

You can't explain it and it might not make any
sense to anyone, but what can you say, you found
an experience that gave you joy. The funny thing
is, most of us have felt that but never even used
that word before. I guarantee you've never heard a
friend say, "That new video game gave me joy!" or
"I drafted the perfect fantasy football team, what
a joy!" It's an uncommon word but a common
feeling.

Right now, if you'd rather use a different word like
"happiness," "thrill," or "excitement," feel free. I don't

care what word you use to describe joy, as long as you're experiencing it in your life.

Joy Works Two Ways

If your Best Moments List was dominated by experiences, you might be a joy person. If that's the case, there are two types of joy you should think about:

1. A joy you *want* to do
2. A joy you *have* to do

In the first one, you find something you love and then do everything you can to get better at it. Brendan Leonard is a great example of a want-to joy because he will never win the New York City Marathon. It's not for lack of trying. Despite titling his book *I Hate Running and You Can Too*, he's a dedicated ultrarunner. One year, for instance, he ran a marathon distance every week. I'm not saying he ran a total of 26.2 miles every week. I'm saying he did a 26.2-mile run every week, or the equivalent of 52 marathons in a year.

He's not going to win the New York City Marathon, though, and you won't either. He's comfortable with that because that's not the point of this endeavor. "You won't ever find yourself telling your grandkids, 'I got 33,789th place that year, but if a couple of things had gone a little differently for me, I could have gotten 32,372nd place,'" he says. "And when you tell your coworkers you ran the New York City Marathon, none of them are going to ask, 'Did you win?'"[1]

Brendan runs for the joy of running. He runs for the challenge. He runs to compete against the version of himself that didn't think he could do it. He runs to get better at that activity, which is a fuel that's every bit as motivating as impact.

George Mallory, the famed mountaineer, summed up joy best when a *New York Times* reporter asked why he wanted to climb Mount Everest: "Because it's there."

Whether you win or lose, whether you ever get to see the impact, whether anyone even knows you did the thing you're doing, you're going to keep doing it because the joy of getting better propels you.

The second type of joy is a have-to joy. That's when you find a way to enjoy something you have to do by making it fun.

For example, I didn't want to take the ACT. Very rarely do I meet a teenager who says, "I can't wait to take the SAT and ACT. There's just something about massive tests that determine my future that really excites me!"

But I had to take it.

Being a teenager is full of have-to moments.

If you want to get your driver's license, you have to practice driving.

If you want to get into college, you have to write essays.

If you want to pass English, you have to put up with some less-than-helpful fellow students in your group project.

In some families, you have to play a sport or you have to work a summer job or you have to babysit your siblings when your parents go to dinner.

We have to deal with a lot of have-tos. To enjoy them a little more, add some joy. To do that, ask yourself questions like this:

Can I do it better?

Can I do it faster?

Can I do it in fewer steps?

Can I do it with a friend?

Can I measure and track my performance?

Can I give myself a small reward when I finish?

Better yet, can I get my parents to pay me after it's over?

That last one is very unique to our season of life. It's weird if you're 35 years old and call your parents to say, "I don't want to do my taxes but I have to. Will you give me $20 if I finish them early?" But as teenagers, we can get away with that.

Why do you think I read so many books in high school? It wasn't because they were assigned to me by teachers. It was because my parents offered to pay me for a reading list. Together we came up with 15 books and then I worked my way through them. I wasn't reading *My Ántonia* and *Great Expectations* at the pool because I'm an amazing student. I was reading them because I found a way to add joy. I had a list I crossed off (measured my performance), I wanted to see how fast I could get through it (tracked my performance), and my parents paid me when it was over (reward).

Will every parent go for that? Maybe not, but I promise you that when you show initiative, there's going to be an adult in your life who shows up to support that.

If you've got a want-to joy right now—like robotics, video games, working at a clothing store because you love fashion, or a million other options—congratulations! Want-to joys are wonderful.

If you've got a have-to task you've been dreading,

congratulations! Adding some joy to it by asking a few questions will make it so much better.

The path is the same in both situations: to get good at something you *want* to do or enjoy something you *have* to do, find a little joy.

Turns Out, It Does Take a Village

I (McRae) have a prediction.

One hundred years from now, there won't be a single scientific study that says isolation is good for teenagers. Doctors won't write articles titled "The Health Benefits of Being Alone in Your Room Without Friends for an Entire Year." Teachers won't suggest eating lunch in your car by yourself as a way to improve high school. Parents won't propose you spend more time looking at your phone and less time laughing with friends at the neighborhood pool.

None of that will happen.

How can I be so confident about something so far

in the future? Because we're already talking about how destructive loneliness is, especially for our generation.

For the first time ever, the Surgeon General of the United States (think of them as the head doctor for the entire country) has laid out a framework to deal with social connection. He warned, "Given the significant health consequences of loneliness and isolation, we must prioritize building social connection the same way we have prioritized health issues such as tobacco, obesity and substance use disorders."[1]

That's a strong statement when you really look at it. Think about how many anti-tobacco and anti-vaping posters you've seen in your school. How many assemblies about the dangers of drugs and alcohol have you attended? I bet your answer is the same as mine—a lot!

Now think about this: How many posters have you seen about the importance of friends? How many assemblies have you been to about forming stronger relationships? I bet the answer is hardly any.

If community is the fuel that moves you the most, let's simplify the whole situation, shove loneliness into a locker, and build the types of relationships that will help the most.

Community Comes in a Four-Pack

How many relationships do you need to have a fun, fantastic life? I wish there was an exact answer, but there's not. I can't say, "With 5.7 friends on average during high school, you're guaranteed to have the best spring breaks." Or "If you have 4.7 adults in your life who care about your future, your senior year will be a lot easier." Community doesn't work that way.

Maybe your Best Moments List was full of relationships because you love helping teach art to younger students at an after-school program. Maybe you're an introvert, but that doesn't mean you like to be lonely. It means you'd rather have one best friend instead of 10 casual friends. Maybe being on the soccer team and having 22 friends united around a singular goal is what fills you up the most. Every teenager is different when it comes to community, but what's the same for all of us is that community tends to come in four varieties.

All of your relationships will fit in one of these four buckets:

1. Family
2. Kids
3. Friends
4. Trusted Adults

Here's how I define each:

Family: Immediate and extended

This is the easiest category to define. Your immediate family is your mom, dad, and siblings. Essentially, this is who you come from. If your grandmother raised you or you have a stepmom you are close with, they're your immediate family too. Counselors sometimes call that your family of origin, which sounds like some sort of Marvel backstory. *My family of origin is from a distant planet made of jade.* Extended family are your cousins, uncles, aunts, nephews, nieces, and so forth. We live on the same street as my Uncle Justin, Aunt Marci, and my two cousins, Addie and Tucker. They are my extended family.

Kids: Anyone who looks up to you

In high school, there's a clear age-based pecking order. A senior is very different from a freshman. A sophomore is different from an eighth grader. When you're our age, there's always someone younger looking up to you. You might not feel that way right now, but I promise it's true. The crazy thing is that younger kids will listen to you faster than they'll listen to adults.

I saw this happen with our neighborhood swim team for years. We had two types of coaches on the team: adults and high schoolers. When a junior in high school pulled aside a fifth grader to give them backstroke advice, they paid attention. When an adult coach did the same exact thing, the kid would zone out a bit. Our opinion really matters to younger kids.

This is why senior year can feel a little awkward at first. There's no one for you to look up to. You're excited to be at the top of the food chain, but you're also a little nervous because now you're in charge. You're the older kid that younger kids are now watching. I (L.E.) felt that when I was put in charge of the trumpet line in our marching band. When freshman students goofed off, just like I had when I was that age, it was now my job to get them back on task.

If you can't easily think of any kids like that in your life, here are a few questions that will help:

Do you have a younger sibling?

Do you have a younger cousin?

Do you have a younger neighbor?

Are there underclassmen in any of the activities you do at school?

Are you in a leadership position in a sport or
after-school job?

If the answer to any of those questions is "yes,"
congratulations—you know some kids.

Friends: People who overlap at least one game

Remember the five games from chapter 9?
School, money, relationships, health, and fun. A
friend is someone you share one of those games
with. It could be school. You have three classes
with Mark and help each other with homework if
you're ever absent. The game could also be health
related. Maybe you run at the same pace as Amy in
cross-country practice and spend half of the miles
talking. The health game of being fast at running
turned you into natural friends. Your friendship
could be related to fun. Maybe you're both obsessed with a video game and play it together each
night.

There are a million ways to become friends and a
million types of friends you can have. For instance,
you may talk with some friends in class but you
don't text each other. Or you're on a group chat with
some friends but wouldn't invite them to your house
for a sleepover. Some friends you'd grab a coffee with

but you wouldn't want to room with them at college. Some friends you'd sit with at lunch but not text if you got your heart broken. They're hangout friends but not "friend" friends.

Did any of that sound complicated? Of course it did, but I guarantee that right now you know exactly what I'm talking about. The funny thing is that the types of friends always confuses my parents. They'll say, "Why don't you have so-and-so over?" and I'll say, "We're more inside-school friends and not outside-school friends." They end up baffled, but I bet you know what I mean.

Trusted Adults: Older people you look up to

I (L.E.) look up to Amy Fenton. She was my small group leader from sixth grade all the way to senior year. (She's also Jadyn's mom from chapter 15.) One of the reasons I chose to attend Samford University was that Amy went there. She took our group to Samford's homecoming one year, and that sealed the deal for me. I fell in love with the campus and the education opportunities, but I was also influenced in my decision by the respect I have for her. There are a handful of other adults I feel the same way about. When I look at them, I think, "That's what I want to be like someday."

What will you admire about an adult you know? It could be that they own a business and you've always wanted to be an entrepreneur too. It could be that they're serious about their health and the marathon medals hanging in their garage are interesting to you. It could be that they seem to laugh a lot with their family and that's something that is missing from your own family. You wish your family could be goofy together like theirs is. It could be that they're wealthy and successful. It could be anything.

A trusted adult is a 3D picture of a future you want to have. The trusted part matters because then you'll actually take their advice. If I trust that someone genuinely has my best in mind, then I'm much more willing to share my life with them and accept feedback on the decisions I'm making.

This last category of community is the smallest for most teenagers. You might have 20 casual friends at school and only one trusted adult. That's perfectly fine.

In the best-case scenario, your parents will fit into the category of trusted adult, but not every teenager lives in a best-case world. If your parents are going through their own issues, don't feel like a failure because they're not in this category for you. Find a teacher, coach, extended family member, boss, or other adult who can help pick up the slack for this role.

Those are the four categories of community. When I was describing them, did anyone instantly come to mind? I bet somebody's name popped into your head. But if you went 0 for 4, don't worry, we can work on that together in the next chapter.

How to Build Your List

What's the best gift you've ever been given?

Maybe it was a Barbie Dreamhouse you wanted when you were six years old.

Maybe it was your first car, which was old and worn out but that didn't matter because it belonged to you.

Maybe it was something sentimental from a grandparent or something unexpected from a friend.

Regardless of what you'd put on your "best gift ever" list, I bet you can think of a few. That's because when people we care about give us something important, we remember it. The same is true with the community you want to build. If relationships are your fuel and you want more of it, the next step is to give the right people the right things.

Family—Give Patience

I (L.E.) have a hard time when McRae gets a cold. I'm not worried about her health—it's just a cold after all. It's the sniffling I have a problem with. And the coughing. And the throat clearing. And the elephant-like nose blowing. And . . . it's an issue. I'm working on it.

It's weird that when McRae catches a cold, I catch a bad attitude. It's even weirder that I don't act that way when my friends get sick. It's odd that I've never once yelled at my friends, "Cough in your elbow!" even though I've said that same thing to McRae a thousand times. Maybe it's not odd, though, because as much as we love our families, they can push our buttons faster than anyone else.

Do you know what you need to give your family when you're a student? Patience. How much? More than you think. How often? More than you'd like. Patience is the glue for strong families, and strong families are fun to be part of. When your younger brother is annoying, give him patience. When your older sister is bossy like a second mom, give her patience. When your dad forgets to ask how your final was, give him patience. When your mom asks you to empty the dishwasher even though it's definitely your sister's turn, give her patience.

Is it easy? Definitely not, but we're too far into this book to pretend that awesome lives don't take any work. Two things will happen if you dare to try this approach:

1. You'll feel better. Overreacting, keeping score, getting even—all those options leave you feeling angry, exhausted, and overwhelmed.

2. They'll give you patience too. It's wild that when we help others, they end up helping us in return. Someone should write something that says "Do unto others as you would have them do unto you."

Practice patience with your family and watch what happens.

Kids—Give Encouragement

Maybe the kid who looks up to you needs advice. Maybe they need guidance. Maybe they need feedback. But do you know what they need way before that? Encouragement. They need someone who is a little further ahead to say, "It's going to be okay" or "Good job" or even "The ACT isn't so bad, don't worry about it."

You might think your words don't have weight, but they do. I saw this firsthand with something my dad used to do at summer camps. Years ago, he spoke to thousands of high school students at beach and mountain camps. In one session, he'd talk specifically to rising seniors and seniors who had already graduated.

His speech was good, but the moment the audience loved the most was when the students who had already finished high school would encourage the new seniors. Teen after teen would stand up in the middle of the crowd and say things like "Don't put pressure on yourself to have a perfect senior year, because there's no such thing." Or "Lean on your friends and don't miss out on chances to spend time with them." Or "Don't coast after you get into college, finish strong." The room grew quiet as students just like you shared encouragement.

You don't have to be a leader to encourage someone. You don't have to be popular. You don't have to know all the answers. You just have to make a little effort and be a little brave.

Give the kids in your community encouragement.

You become
**BETTER
FRIENDS**
with people you
spend time with.

JON ACUFF

#HowTeensWin

Friends—Give Time

Every friendship runs on one simple principle: *you become better friends with people you spend time with.* This is especially true when you're a student because time is one of the only resources we have to invest.

You don't have a lot of money when you're our age. You don't have as much freedom as you'll have in your 20s. You might not have a car or even a job yet. But do you know what you do have? Time. If you want more friends, spend more time with more people. If you want deeper friendships, spend more time with a small handful of people. What could that look like? Here are a few examples:

- Play Xbox with a friend.
- Volunteer to give a neighbor a ride to school in the morning. (Saving a friend from the high school bus is one of the kindest things you can do.)
- FaceTime a friend while you're doing home-work and finish it together.
- Go on a run with a friend on the wrestling team who is also looking to train in the offseason.

- Invite a friend to join you on a family vacation.
- Text a friend who missed a day of school and ask if they need the homework.
- Go to the movies with a group of friends.

Those are just seven examples of perhaps seven billion possible ways you can spend time with friends. If you ever find that some healthy solitude is turning into some unhealthy loneliness, turn to the one resource you have more than any other—time.

Friendships run on time.

Trusted Adults—Give Questions

If you want to shock an adult, ask them for help.

Younger generations like ours often get labeled as entitled, disconnected from the real world, and sad. That couldn't be further from the truth. I think we're hungry, hopeful, and hardworking. The best way to show that to a trusted adult and to receive some wisdom in the process is to ask a question. You don't have to climb to the top of a mountain and ask a guru for the meaning of life, but what if you asked your mom for a few tips on picking a college major? I bet she'd be thrilled to help you!

It's hard being a teenager. You can certainly learn a ton on YouTube, but a trusted adult can also fill in a lot of the knowledge gaps. When my friend wanted to install a new light switch in his bedroom, he watched a video. It was really helpful, but the videographer forgot to mention that you need to turn the power off in your house before you get started. He was about to electrocute himself until he talked with his dad. One question was all it took to realize the breaker needed to be flipped.

Let's change the world and save ourselves from burning down the house by asking a few questions of the people ahead of us.

Give trusted adults questions.

The Future Is Intentional Community

If you ask 100 people what their goals are, 99 of them won't even mention community. Most people think that relationships just sort of happen all on their own. Maybe that's the way it was in the 1950s when you had to drive to an office to work, talk to a grocer to get your food, and buy a paper from a newsstand. But you and I could live a complete life without ever leaving our houses and never seeing a single person except for the Uber Eats driver.

If we want community these days, it has to be intentional.

Most people won't put patience, encouragement, time, or questions into their communities, but we're not most people. We're students who are going to have strong relationships, and we're starting today.

The Stories We Tell Ourselves

To the average person, the bracelets on my arm don't seem like they're worth anything. They're not made of gold. They don't have diamonds on them. They aren't from a designer with an Italian-sounding name. If anything, they look like an over-enthusiastic kindergartner in love with pastel colors made them quickly. But to me they're priceless. The reason why is simple—Taylor Swift.

These aren't just bracelets, these are the treasures I (McRae) traded for at the Taylor Swift concert in Nashville, Tennessee. I don't care if other people think they look silly and cheap. When I see them,

I'm reminded of one of the best moments of my entire life.

That's what stuff does to you. We talked about how wins, experiences, and relationships translate into fuels to keep us motivated as we work on goals, but what about stuff? What about all the physical items we put on our Best Moments List? How can they drive us forward?

The answer is simple—with a story.

The Five Stories

I don't know how many items on your list would qualify as stuff, but I do know one thing—none of it is there by accident. You added stuff to that list because it matters to you, and it matters to you because it tells a story.

Take L.E.'s list, for example. Item 17 is an old sweatshirt. It's not expensive. It's not rare. It's not even that well made. (Sorry, L.E., it's true.) The reason it's on the list is that it's not an ordinary sweatshirt. It's my mom's sorority sweatshirt from college. When L.E. also became a Chi-O, that sweatshirt became significant. It no longer just kept her warm, it told a story. Every bit of stuff on your list does the same thing. Fortunately, the stories aren't a mystery you have to figure out on your own. There are only five you need to know.

Story 1: This stuff makes me feel nostalgic.

Other than arms, a sweatshirt can't really hold much. It's not a bucket, bag, or box. But it does hold memories. There is stuff on your list that tells a particular story about a moment in time. The water bottle from camp. The mouthguard you wore when you first made the football team. The seashell from visiting your aunt and uncle at the beach. Each of these items reminds you of a best moment.

There are trillions of shells on every beach. The one you picked up on an empty Thanksgiving seashore, the one you somehow managed to bring home without breaking, the one you look at when everyday life feels dull and not very "beachy"—that's a memory. That's a story that inspires you to keep moving forward. Are there any items on your list like that?

Story 2: This stuff makes me feel successful.

The playbill from your high school performance isn't just 12 pieces of poorly printed paper held together by two sad staples. It's a story about the role you auditioned for, rehearsed for, and crushed! You did it. You didn't let the stage fright win this time. You beat it, and when you finally took your last bow at the show, you felt so accomplished. That playbill made your list because it makes you feel successful. You never brag about it to friends or make a big deal about it at dinner with your family, but it's on your nightstand for a reason.

If you doubt how much I believe in the power of stories like this, you haven't seen the back of my bedroom door. I have taped up a collection of items dating back to the fifth grade. For the last seven years I've been collecting swim ribbons, honor society certificates, and yes, even my Grizzly All-Star award I got in the fifth grade for being helpful in gym class. I know most of those things just look like pieces of paper, but every time I see them they make me feel successful.

What do you own that makes you feel like you owned a moment?

Story 3: This stuff makes me feel inspired.

I can't look at my watercolor paint set without wanting to paint. Jeremy Johnson, an 18-year-old boy in my neighborhood, can't look at a basketball without wanting to dribble and shoot it. Some stuff makes you feel inspired to take action. A new pair of running shoes makes you feel inspired . . . to run. Crazy, right? Truly mind-blowing stuff.

I think that's why my dad is so obsessed with notebooks. Opening a crisp, brand-new notebook makes him want to write. He wants to fill those pages.

How about you? Is there anything on your list that makes you feel inspired? This particular story makes it easy to see why stuff can be a good fuel. If a cheap set of watercolors inspires me to paint and my goal is to finish my portfolio project for art class, guess what I probably need to keep on the top of my desk? My paint set! Seeing it every day when I get ready for school will give me the boost I need to get started on my goal.

Story 4: This stuff makes me feel cool.

Are Jordans the best shoes that have ever been made? Are the materials different from other shoes? Can you run faster or jump higher in them? Not really, but they're cool. Same with jeans. Does it make sense to pay more for jeans that have big rips and tears in them? From a practical standpoint, is that smart? Maybe not, but they're cool. You probably can't explain some of the items on your list. They don't offer much function. They're expensive. They might be fragile or small and easy to lose. But none of that matters because they're cool.

If an adult teases you about something you desperately want, remind them that Golden Goose sneakers are expensive, lots of coolers will keep things as cold as a Yeti, and a Big Green Egg isn't the only way to grill a hamburger. Everyone, regardless of their age, wants to feel cool.

Story 5: This stuff makes me feel connected.

There are objects you own that make you feel like you're in a community. My mom's old sorority sweatshirt is a quick example of that. It makes L.E. feel connected to my mom and everyone else who is in the sorority. A woman in her 60s saw her wearing it at the post office and exclaimed, "Me too! I wish I remembered our secret handshake."

The connection can be one-on-one, something you share with a good friend, or even an item that ties you to a large group. I have a necklace that everyone from my cabin at camp wears. Outside of the 15 girls who shared a summer in Black Mountain, North Carolina, that necklace doesn't mean much, but inside our group it's special. It reminds us all of a shared experience that no one can take away.

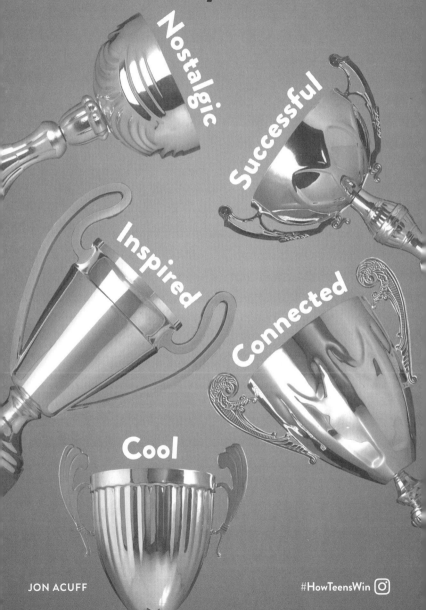

Do you know any adults who own Jeeps? They wave at each other on the road. Not only that, but they give each other ducks as mementos. You'll come back from dinner to find a bright yellow rubber ducky on your door handle from a stranger who saw your Jeep in the parking lot and wanted to encourage you. A Jeep isn't a vehicle, it's a 5,000-pound story. It's a connection.

Those are the five stories your stuff tells, but here's where it gets really fun. Now that you know the type of stuff you care about the most, you can add more of it to your life going forward. That's the type of self-awareness it often takes adults decades to learn, but you're figuring it out in a matter of minutes.

For example, if 80 percent of the stuff on your list made you feel inspired, guess what you need to focus on to stay motivated? Inspiration. Get a notebook, get a colored pencil set, get a new football. Deliberately ask for birthday presents that are going to light you up.

If, on the other hand, you do a quick survey of your room and realize the stuff that matters most to you makes you feel successful, guess what will help you in the future? Stuff tied to success. Is there a college you really want to go to in a few years? Request a brochure and put a page from it on your bedroom wall. Write the name of the school in dry erase marker on your bathroom mirror. Ask for a hoodie from the school for Christmas. On the days you don't want to put in any effort, you'll be surrounded by stuff that keeps you going.

Is a T-shirt just a T-shirt sometimes? Sure, we all own things that are just things. But often the life we have can be made so much better by the people—and yes, even the stuff—we fill it with.

Pick yours on purpose.

The Four Fuels

From stories and community to joy and impact, the four fuels will drive you to achieve the goals you want. But they're not the only fuels that exist. There are negative forms as well. For example, did your parents ever talk to you about peer pressure? That's a type of fuel too. We've all had moments where we look back on a bad decision and wonder, "Why did I do that?" Often, the reason is we were using a toxic fuel.

We felt peer pressure.

We wanted to fit in.

We hoped people would like us if we went along with the plan, no matter how dumb the plan seemed to us on the inside.

Later, when we reflect on the mistake we made, it almost feels like we were being pushed along, right up until that fuel brought us to destinations we really didn't want, like detention, being grounded, or failing classes.

Fuel as a motivator goes both ways. When it's positive, you end up with success. When it's negative, you end up with regrets.

My friend's dad found out what happens when you use the wrong fuel when he once accidentally put diesel fuel in his car's gas tank. It was a stressful day, he wasn't paying attention, and when the engine seized up as he pulled away from the gas station, he knew he'd made a serious mistake.

More than $3,000 later, the engine was fixed and my friend had learned a valuable lesson—always put in the right fuel.

Do you know which of the four fuels motivates you the most? Do you know what your "right fuel" is?

I do.

I could tell you that answer right now if you showed me your Best Moments List.

Impact is a win. The world is different because of something you did. That's the very best type of fuel.

Joy is an experience. The effort you put in was worth it because of the joy you experienced from doing it.

Community is a relationship. The people are what made the moment a best moment. The promise of more community will keep you going when the goal gets challenging.

Finally, the right stuff always tells a story.

If you want to know what fuel will drive you tomorrow, just look back at what your list taught you about yesterday. Make a quick tally of your wins, experiences, relationships, and stuff. Did you have 30 wins, 20 experiences, 15 items of stuff, and 5 relationships? Then the two fuels that will help you the most are impact and joy.

I'm personally driven by community. Running cross-country is hard, sweaty, tiring work most days. But knowing other girls, going to lunch with fellow runners, and cheering each other on, that's why I do it. I haven't won a race. That's not why I do it though. I do it for the community.

Want to know what fuel will drive you tomorrow? Look back at what your list taught you about yesterday.

You and I will probably use different fuels in different ways, but the end result will be the same: more time spent in the Potential Zone. We also won't use just one fuel but will benefit from all four at some point in our lives.

When you start to use the four fuels more deliberately and spend more time in your Potential Zone, a funny thing happens: The future is no longer intimidating. The years after high school don't seem daunting but promising. You're not waiting until your mid-20s or early 30s to wake up to what's possible. You already know!

You've knocked out a few Easy Goals and broken out of your Comfort Zone. You've avoided the Chaos Zone with some Middle Goals. Now you're ready to answer the question we've talked about for this entire book:

How do I live in the Potential Zone full-time?

Visiting for an hour or two won't be enough for you once you get an idea of what you're really capable of.

How do you make your home there?

How do you open every gift you have?

How do you live out of your full potential?

With Guaranteed Goals.

Guarantee Your Success

I (L.E.) am going to graduate from college in 2026 with a degree in accounting.

Before I turn 22, I will have published two books.

By the time I am 25, I will have more in my 401K than the average 35-year-old.

By the end of the year, McRae will have run 300 miles.

By the time she goes to college, she'll have $15,000 saved up.

By the time she finishes her summer, she will have 350 hours of community service that will look great on her college applications.

At this point, I bet it sounds like we're some sort of goal-obsessed family who all get up at 4 a.m. to work out together while shouting positive affirmations at each other. I promise, though, our house isn't that hardcore. My dad just feels like he didn't make the most of his high school years. He knows he could have had more fun, more friends, and more success if he just had the right tools. He talks to us about them a lot so that we can take advantage of them a lot earlier in life than he did.

One of those tools is Guaranteed Goals, and it's the reason I'm so confident about those goals McRae and I are working on.

The Painfully Obvious Magic of Guaranteed Goals

Easy Goals get us out of the Comfort Zone.

Middle Goals help us avoid the Chaos Zone.

And Guaranteed Goals? They help us stay in the Potential Zone.

The best news in the entire book is that Guaranteed Goals run on the resource you and I both have—time.

How can I guarantee that by age 25 I'll have more in my 401K than the average 35-year-old? Because by that point I will have worked on that goal for more than 10 years. You can accomplish almost anything if you take small steps toward it over a big amount of time.

You can accomplish almost anything if you take small steps toward it over a big amount of time.

JON ACUFF

#HowTeensWin

I know a 17-year-old who built a six-figures-a-year photography business by taking photos at our school's football games. Could she turn it into her full-time career? Absolutely. So could you with a Guaranteed Goal.

The problem is that nobody thinks goals can be guaranteed, so let's define what we mean by a Guaranteed Goal before we jump into how to build one.

A Guaranteed Goal is a goal where the efforts ensure the results. If you put in the work, it's impossible for you to lose. If you lean in to the process, the progress always follows. If you give it time, the reward always happens. That's the magic of Guaranteed Goals, and it's always painfully obvious.

How does McRae know and not just hope that by the end of the year she will have run 300 miles? Because if she stays faithful to cross-country practice, that's a guarantee. If she consistently runs 15 miles a week, she can accomplish that goal in six months, never mind a whole year.

How do I know that by the time I'm 25 I'll have more in my 401K than the average 35-year-old? Because I have proof. That's the best part about the goal ladder from chapter 11. It doesn't just give you progress for your goal, it gives you evidence that you're capable of even more.

A few years ago, I started working for my dad's small company. I'm an employee and began saving the money I earned into a 401K. It wasn't a lot at first, but it doesn't have to be a lot when you start at 15.

I did some easy financial goals that were simple to accomplish. Then he helped me grow them a little. The Middle Goals weren't too bad either. Now that I've climbed the goal ladder a few rungs, the top goal of financial freedom when I'm older doesn't feel that impossible. In fact, it feels guaranteed.

The wins you get with your Easy Goals become evidence that you're ready for Middle Goals. The wins you get with your Middle Goals become proof that you're ready for Guaranteed Goals. You don't have to guess if it's time to level up some part of your life. The results make it obvious.

You don't need a cool, tall dad to make it happen either. (See if you can figure out which two words my dad added to that last sentence.) Anyone can climb the goal ladder. My friend Callie saved up $35,000 by working at her local pool. She wasn't going to wait and see if she could afford college. She started figuring that out for herself in the ninth grade. After all, we are the "figure it out" generation.

We are the "figure it out" generation.

We have more access to more information and opportunity than any other generation that has ever lived. Are things perfect? Nope, but right now I'm 20 years old, which means I'm three years older than my great-grandfather was when he joined the Army to go to Germany and drive tanks against the Nazis. That helps me keep things in perspective when people try to tell me my generation has it so hard. We might not have it easy, but we can figure it out. That's what we do.

We edit videos on our phone with the technical expertise that would have taken a semester of film school 20 years ago.

We make music in our bedroom that would have taken a studio full of equipment 20 years ago.

We write code, create websites, and build robots that would have taken a degree in computer science 20 years ago.

We figure it out. That's what we do.

If you're ready to figure out a few Guaranteed Goals for your life, make sure they have these five factors.

1. Guaranteed Goals have extended time frames, usually 90 days to a year.

If that feels like a long time to you, that's only be-cause it is a long time. It's also why you don't start with Guaranteed Goals, you work your way up to Guaranteed Goals. If my parents told me on day one of taking piano lessons, "You're going to play piano for the next 10 years," I would have felt trapped, not encouraged. If on day one of high school band I knew it would take three years to become line leader, that would have been overwhelming. If my guidance counselor told me it would take a whole semester to get ready for the ACT, that would have been demoralizing.

But all I did was play piano for a few weeks as an Easy Goal. When I realized I liked it, a few weeks turned into a few months, which was a Middle Goal. Ten years later, when I was packing a keyboard to keep under my bed in college, I realized I had a Guaranteed Goal on my hands. The goal was now "play piano at college as a way to relieve stress." I had to work my way up to that because when I first learned to play, the piano didn't cure stress, it caused it! It was awkward and difficult to learn all the notes. Now, though, because I've practiced so long, it's a source of comfort to me.

For band, I went to the weeklong summer camp as a freshman. That was an Easy Goal. I practiced for months, a Middle Goal, and then ended up being the line leader my senior year, a Guaranteed Goal.

For the ACT, I took a practice test one week. That was an Easy Goal. I started studying consistently for it, a Middle Goal. Eventually I spent four months in a prep class at school, a Guaranteed Goal. By the time I took the ACT, I was guaranteed to do better than if I hadn't put in all that work.

The time passed for each of those goals, my actions stacked up, and before I knew it, I was enjoying some really fun accomplishments.

Saving up for your first car isn't an Easy Goal. That's going to take longer than a week. Saving up for your first car isn't even a Middle Goal. That's probably going to take longer than 90 days. Saving up for your first car is a Guaranteed Goal. It might take you six months or a year to finish, but if you keep at it, there's no way you're going to be riding the bus senior year. That's a guarantee.

2. Guaranteed Goals are 100 percent in your control.

If you put in real effort, the results are math, not a miracle. This is perhaps the most misunderstood part of Guaranteed Goals. For example, you don't control whether you get accepted to a specific college. There are too many factors outside your control. If you live out of state from the University of Georgia or the University of Southern California, that makes it dramatically harder to get in. You don't control how many students apply the year you apply. If 10,000 applied one year but 20,000 apply the year you do, your odds just got twice as long. You don't control if the school's football team wins a national championship and students from other states are suddenly interested in attending. There are a thousand different factors outside of your control.

But you do control your grades in high school. You do control your test scores. You do control the quality and quantity of your extracurriculars. You do control your community service hours. You do control if you apply the first day applications are accepted. You do control if you work with a tutor at school to get extra help in tough classes. You do control asking people to write letters of recommendation. You have more control than you think.

Here are a few examples of goals you control versus goals you don't control.

You control: Playing a specific sport
You don't control: Making a specific team

If you want to play goalie for your high school soccer team but an amazing goalie from California moves to your district, you don't control making that team. You do control playing with a traveling team, at the local YMCA, or in a pickup game at the park on Saturdays. You control playing soccer because there are a million ways to do that.

You control: Dating
You don't control: Dating a specific person
    If you ask enough people on a date, you are going to go on a date. But, as much as it pains me to say this, that specific person might say no.

You control: Applying for scholarships
You don't control: Earning every scholarship
    My friend applied for an athletic scholarship that was focused on overcoming adversity. The same year she did, a school near us flooded and lost every bit of football equipment they had. The athletes on that team had to rebuild their entire program, and our community rallied around them. They had a dramatic, true story of adversity. My friend had a good application essay but didn't have a shot at that particular scholarship.
    In situations like that, you control your actions, not your outcomes. (She ended up getting a full

ride with other scholarships because she didn't quit applying.)

3. Guaranteed Goals are easy to measure.

I started this chapter with six Guaranteed Goals:

- I am going to graduate from college in 2026 with a degree in accounting.
- Before I turn 22, I will have published two books.
- By the time I am 25, I will have more in my 401K than the average 35-year-old.
- By the end of the year, McRae will have run 300 miles.
- By the time McRae goes to college, she'll have $15,000 saved up.
- By the time McRae finishes her summer, she will have 350 hours of community service that will look great on her college applications.

Do you notice what they all have in common?

There's a number associated with each one of them. If you can't easily track your Guaranteed Goals, you'll get bored. When that happens, you'll either start another goal, which is Chaos Zone behavior, or you'll give up, which lands you right back in the Comfort Zone.

How could we make the example goals I mentioned under point 2 even better? By making them easier to measure. For the soccer goal, you could say, "I will find three teams in my community that don't require tryouts. I will contact each one of them by November 15." Ohhhh, now we've got two numbers—three teams and November 15. This just got real!

For the dating example, you could say, "I will ask four people to homecoming." Is that a weird goal? A little bit, but if you didn't get to go to homecoming last year and you really want to go this year, it would be weirder to do nothing.

And for the last example, the scholarship, that's the easiest goal of all to measure. Say, "I will apply for 10 scholarships by September 1." Each time you apply for one, cross it off your list. I guarantee you'll feel great each time you do.

The more measurable your goal is, the more likely you'll achieve it.

4. Guaranteed Goals force you to be more deliberate.

Do you think Steph Curry plays basketball casually? Do you think it's kind of like a hobby he does and

The more
MEASURABLE
your goal is,
the more
likely you'll
achieve it.

when he's not playing in games he's just somewhere relaxing?

When you watch him in the NBA Finals, it's impossible to think he's lazy. Just in case I was wrong, though, I double-checked with an NBA trainer. David Nurse has trained dozens of NBA players for years. He estimates that Curry has put in 26,462.5 hours of practice (2.5 hours per day × 365 days per year from age 6 to age 35). If you practiced one hour a day it would take you 72.5 years to accumulate that same amount of time. Big goals take big effort. That's always how it goes.

When it comes to time and your goals, here's a simple way to break it down:

Easy Goals require 1 percent of your week, or about two hours.

Middle Goals require 3 percent of your week, or about five hours.

Guaranteed Goals require 5 percent of your week, or about eight hours.

If that seems like a lot, flip the way you're looking at it.

You're not saying, "I have to spend eight hours a week on my goal." You're saying, "I get to spend eight hours a week doing something I love."

Find a goal you love so much that Netflix becomes boring.

When you find a Guaranteed Goal you really enjoy doing, other stuff starts to look boring. Have you ever forgotten to eat because you were having so much fun playing a video game? Have you ever been surprised when it was already time to go home from the lake because you were enjoying wakesurfing with your friends and didn't even notice the sun was about to go down? Have you ever lost track of time because you were scrolling Instagram?

You've already experienced this principle before, and now you can make it work for you. When you get locked into a big goal, other things in your life seem small and insignificant. You'll naturally want to make time for the goal. My crazy hope for you is that you find a goal you love so much that Netflix becomes boring.

5. Guaranteed Goals sound impossible when you tell people about them.

Have you ever been discouraged by someone's reaction to your goal or dream? We all have. I remember when someone insulted my plan to be in the high school marching band. I don't know if I've ever seen my mom so mad. It's hard enough to be a teenager, and it only gets harder when someone criticizes your hope. But with this final point, I'm about to turn that experience upside down.

A Guaranteed Goal is going to stretch you, which means it's also going to stretch some people's belief that you can accomplish it. When you tell a friend an Easy Goal, they should say, "Is that all?" When you tell a friend a Middle Goal, they should say, "Good for you!" When you tell a friend a Guaranteed Goal, they should say, "Are you sure?" A good Guaranteed Goal should sound too weird, too ambitious, or too impossible to other people.

"I'm going to spend 30 days in a canoe going from the Cumberland River in Nashville, Tennessee, to Dauphin Island in the Gulf of Mexico" probably sounds like way too big of a goal to most people, but that's exactly what Luke Saulters did. I can't imagine going 800 miles downriver, avoiding barges that could sink you and sleeping on muddy, mosquito-infested banks when the night finally got so dark you couldn't navigate. I can't imagine any of that, but Luke and his two friends imagined it—and then they actually did it.

I bet a lot of people thought it was impossible.

I bet a lot of people thought it was silly. But when the river collided with the ocean and they finally made it, I bet all three boys knew it was worth it. They also rode their bikes from their neighborhood in Nashville to the Alamo in San Antonio, Texas, so I wouldn't ever bet against these adolescent adventurers.

There's tremendous freedom when your mission isn't to convince everyone that you can accomplish a goal but instead to get people to doubt you. While it's exhausting to get buy-in from people, it's fun to get buy-out. The next time someone doubts you— especially if they're not a friend or trusted adult— pause for a second and think to yourself, "Maybe I'm on the right track."

I Learned This When I Overheard Some Shouting

Is there a law that says our parents have to scream when they talk on the phone? Am I the only one with a dad who feels like he has to shout when he's on a call? I know he's not angry, but when we're in the car and he takes a call, it's like he's trying to reach the other person by yelling out the window to wherever they are instead of using his phone. Do your parents do that too? Please tell me they do.

Phone call yelling is probably what inspired my dad to also yell on podcasts. Even with noise-canceling headphones, if I'm on the same floor of the house he is when he's got a podcast interview, I HEAR EVERY SINGLE WORD.

When his book *All It Takes Is a Goal* came out and he did a podcast tour, I got a literal earful of the ideas in it. The one he shouted—sorry, "talked"—about the most was Guaranteed Goals. The majority of the podcast interviewers just couldn't believe that someone could guarantee a goal. At which point my dad would say, "I couldn't have written about Guaranteed Goals in my first book, but this is my ninth. I write books using these principles. I know you can guarantee big goals because that's how I write my books."

Books aren't magic—or, as my dad shouted a dozen times, "BOOKS AREN'T MAGIC, THEY ARE GOALS, AND GOALS CAN BE GUARANTEED!"

He's right. He recently turned in his tenth book and is already hard at work on his eleventh. He's not just hoping he'll finish it, he has already guaranteed he will to a whole building full of people in Michigan. (That's where his publisher is based.)

If goals are that simple, why doesn't everybody do it?

That's the question, right? If all you have to do to live in your full potential is pick a game, turn it into an Easy Goal, then transform it into a Middle Goal and eventually a Guaranteed Goal, why do 92 percent of all New Year's resolutions fail? Why do most people miss out on most of the goals they care about?

Because they don't have a scorecard.

Create a Scorecard
to Know You're Winning

I (McRae) think one of the worst feelings in the world is to look at photos of an event you weren't invited to. Has that ever happened to you? Maybe it was an accident. Your friends thought you were out of town so they didn't include you in a movie night, but you were home. You could have gone but didn't know about it. And when they all posted about "Best night ever!" you felt hurt.

Before you know it, you're not just looking at the one photo you saw. You're like a detective studying each picture from each friend who was there. You're trying to piece together the whole night, the invite list, and the possible reasons you could have been excluded. Did you say the wrong thing at lunch? Is someone mad at you? What else have they been doing without you?

Have you ever done that? No? Okay, me either then.

Social media is amazing. I feel like our generation is growing up in the golden age of memes. I love how I can connect with friends. I love how I can follow a Taylor Swift concert in a city I've never been to via Instagram videos from a person I've never met. I love it all . . . except comparison.

It's the hardest part of social media.

It's so easy to compare your weekend, your car, your vacation, your clothes, your entire life to someone else's and then come up short. We know we shouldn't do it. Of course we know—our parents constantly encourage us not to.

"It's not real life," they say.

"Take a break from social media for a little bit," they beg.

"Mute the people you have a hard time following," they suggest.

Those words are easy to say but hard to live. And the truth is, our parents didn't have to deal with what we're going through. They didn't have social media when they were our age and probably would have gotten just as stuck.

How do we save ourselves from comparison? The answer is a lot simpler than you think, and it starts by dealing with a different question you probably haven't asked before.

"WHY do I compare myself to other people?"

The Answer

The reason you compare yourself to others is that your brain wants to know that you're making progress in life.

That's it. That's the answer. At times, this feeling might look like insecurity, fear, or jealousy, but the root of comparison is your brain trying to answer the basic question "How are we doing?"

Can you blame it?

Do you remember when you were little and your family would go on a road trip? What's the number one question you would ask over and over again?

"Are we there yet?"

Your parents would get annoyed, but you couldn't help it. We want to know where we're headed. We want to be able to check in on our progress. We want to know the score, especially when it comes to the five big games of school, money, relationships, health, and fun.

Am I in the right classes? Is school always going

to be this hard? Will I get to go to college? Am I supposed to know what I want to major in by now?

Will I have money for college? What about a car? Can I afford to go on spring break this year? When can I get a new phone? Is there a different job that would pay more after school?

How about my relationships? What's the score there? Do I have any real friends? Will there be a spot for me in the cafeteria? Did that person really say that about me? Does everyone get lonely like this, or is everybody else somewhere having an amazing time without me?

How is my health? Am I in shape? Am I out of shape? Does it matter at my age? When will I ever get taller? Is this the body I'll always have?

Am I having fun right now? Everybody says it's hard to be a teenager—is that true? I used to love that hobby in middle school, but I haven't done it for a year. What happened? Does anyone else at my school like K-pop? What would I do for fun if I felt like no one was watching or judging me?

Your brain is constantly curious about your progress, and so are you. You wouldn't work hard at soccer practice for a year if your coach didn't give you updates. You'd get frustrated at school if your teacher said, "I'm not going to tell you your grade until the end of the semester. I won't grade papers, tests, or quizzes for four months, so you'll never know how you're really doing until the last day of school." Your parents wouldn't let you go on fall break with a friend who wouldn't say where you were going, how you were getting there, and how long you were staying. They want information. So do you. So do I.

When our parents ask us things like "How's school?" or "How are you feeling?" or "How are your friendships?" many of us offer vague answers if we offer any.

"It's fine." "I don't know." "I have friends."

That's not good enough for your brain though. Vague answers won't satisfy the most curious part of your body. In that moment, your brain doesn't stop looking for progress updates on your life. It just says, "Okay, if you won't tell me the score, I'll go look at someone else's scorecard and see if I can figure it out that way." That's how comparison starts.

In the absence of a scorecard, your brain will use someone else's. That's a big problem because when you score your life against someone else's scorecard, you will always come up lacking. That's an even bigger temptation for us than it was for our parents because in addition to being the "figure it out" generation we're also the "live vicariously through other people" generation.

For example, when my dad was a kid, he only had two options when it came to playing his Nintendo: play by himself or invite his best friend Dave Bruce over to play. Know what he couldn't do? Watch a four-hour Twitch of someone else playing. He couldn't go on YouTube and watch a two-hour video of a gamer in Phoenix playing *Fortnite*. He could maybe watch an older kid play *Galaga* at the roller-skating rink, but he'd get bored pretty quickly of peering over his shoulder because it was a lot more fun to play the game himself.

Now, though, we spend a lot of our lives watching other people live their lives.

There's no shame in that. Twitch can be awesome. A travel influencer on Instagram can show you countries you've never been to. A YouTube car collector can inspire you to own your own sports car someday. But when comparison rears its ugly head, we no longer get joy from those experiences but

In the absence of a scorecard, your brain will use someone else's.

self-judgment. In that moment, the only thing that will overcome your temptation to compare yourself to other people is having your own scorecard to look at.

What Really Matters

There have been about a billion different tools, techniques, and tricks in this book, but this final one is going to be the simplest. If you were worried I was going to teach you some complicated way to build a scorecard, fear not. There are only three questions to think about:

1. What matters to me?
2. Am I doing it?
3. Could I do it more?

Easy, right?

Take any of the five games—school, money, relationships, health, fun—and apply those questions whenever you feel tempted to compare.

Take school, for example. I (McRae) took orchestra senior year. That wouldn't have been a big deal except I had never taken a music lesson in high school. I had never played an instrument. I didn't know how to read music. I couldn't sing or really even clap on beat. So why did I sign up for the class?

Because I knew I would enjoy it. Joy is a big motivator for me. I knew that even if I had to stand in the back for the winter performance and just bang three keys on an old keyboard, I didn't care. It would be fun to me.

Those last two words are critical: *to me.*

My scorecard is *my* scorecard. I didn't judge the decision to sign up for orchestra based on anyone else's life, just my own. I didn't even tell my parents I was doing it. I just came home after the first day of school senior year and declared, "I changed one of my classes to orchestra!"

"But you don't know how to play an instrument."

"I know," I replied. "But it will be fun."

I started calling it a "side quest," that unexpected moment where a character in a video game does a small mission that's off the beaten path from the main objective.

L.E., a serious musician who has played multiple instruments for more than 10 years, was a bit horrified at my decision. She thought I'd be embarrassed at my lack of ability in the class. I wasn't, though, because my scorecard is different.

When I asked those three questions, here are the answers I got:

1. What matters to me?
    Having fun in my classes, especially senior year.
2. Am I doing it?
    No, the AV class I originally signed up for didn't seem fun.
3. Could I do it more?
    Yes, I could sign up for orchestra!

I didn't sit down with a chart and a notebook to check a million boxes in a difficult decision matrix. I just checked in with me, thought for a little bit, and gave myself permission to make a different choice.

The type of friendships you want will be different from other people's.

My relationships scorecard says "Have as many friends as possible."

L.E.'s says "Have a few close, deep friendships."

We're different, and the same is true for all the other games.

My friend Katie's money scorecard says "Getting your nails done is worth saving up for."

I'd never spend $50 on my nails, but that's okay

because she'd never save up for Taylor Swift tickets like I did.

My health scorecard says "Running is a great way to stay in shape."

My friend Lilly's scorecard says "Running is torture. Swimming is the greatest sport ever invented."

Game by game, it's easy to see the differences between people's scorecards if you look. What if the next time you're comparing yourself to someone else, you were to ask those three questions instead?

1. What matters to me?
2. Am I doing it?
3. Could I do it more?

It's a good life lesson in general, but it's extra important when you're climbing the goal ladder.

Do you know how adults end up in careers they don't like or cities they should have left or relationships that don't fulfill them? As they worked on their goals, they never checked their scorecard.

If interacting with lots of people matters to you and you pick a job that's solitary, guess what you get? An unhappy career.

If travel is what matters to you but you spend all your money on clothes because that's what your

To build
a simple
scorecard,
ask three
questions:

**What matters
to me?**

**Am I
doing it?**

**Could I do
it more?**

friends do, guess what you get? An unhappy savings account.

If you love dancing and hate running but feel like running is the only "real way" to stay in shape, guess what you get? An unhappy relationship with exercise.

The good news is that we get to choose.

We get to decide.

We get to be deliberate.

We get to pick.

And picking the things that will make you the happiest long-term is a lot easier when you have a scorecard.

CONCLUSION

(L.E.) am going to London.

Not just for a few days.

Not just for a week or even a month.

I am going to London to study for an entire semester. For four months I'll ride the Tube, commute past Big Ben, and spend long weekends in Scotland or France.

Like anything significant in life, it didn't happen overnight. I knew in sixth grade that I wanted to study abroad. I knew in ninth grade what kind of grades it would take to get into college. I knew in my first year of college what classes I'd need to take to make sure my diploma lined up with the London program. And each step of the way I kept climbing my goal ladder.

I probably won't send you a postcard from

Buckingham Palace because I don't know your address, but if I did, I know what it would say. I know what advice I'd give you about chasing goals as a teenager.

Read this book in reverse.

No one dreams about Easy Goals. I certainly didn't. In sixth grade I didn't say, "I want to read a book about England!" or "All I want to accomplish is watching a TV show about the Queen." Nobody dreams that small.

No one says things like "I want to walk a quarter mile!" or "I want to write 100 words!" or "I want to learn the G chord on a guitar!" or "I want to understand 10 Italian words!"

We all dream much bigger than that about our potential, and we should. We say:

I want to run a marathon!

I want to write a novel!

I want to be the lead guitarist in a band!

I want to move to Italy!

We have massive goals that we know take small steps, but how do we translate big dreams into micro actions? That's the gap where most people give up. Most people find it impossible to break a huge hope

Most people find it impossible to break a huge hope into daily deeds.

into daily deeds. Most people find it difficult to turn potential into a goal. But we're not most people. We're going to accomplish that by going back down the goal ladder we just climbed up in the previous chapters.

Just start with one of the five games: school, money, relationships, health, or fun. Which of those five sounds like it would be a blast to pursue right now? Don't pick the perfect one, just pick the first one that comes to mind.

Once you've got a game in mind, all you have to do is turn it into a Guaranteed Goal. Make sure your Guaranteed Goal

1. Has an extended time frame (90 days to one year)
2. Is 100 percent in your control
3. Is easy to measure
4. Encourages you to be deliberate with your schedule (eight hours of work a week)
5. Sounds impossible when you tell people

If you can save up for a car for a year, if you're in control of applying to part-time jobs until you get one, if you can measure the amount of money you're saving, if you can clear your schedule for at least eight hours of work a week, and if friends think it's impossible, you're on the right track.

Then take your Guaranteed Goal and make it more manageable by shrinking it into a Middle Goal. Make sure your Middle Goal

1. Has a reasonable time frame (30 to 90 days)
2. Is flexible
3. Doesn't fall apart if you miss a day
4. Encourages you to adjust your schedule (five hours of work a week)
5. Takes a little bit of help from a friend or trusted adult

If you can commit to saving money for 30 days, if you're able to focus on it in a variety of ways, if you're willing to forgive yourself if you blow $20 on Taco Bell when you've got food at home, if you can find time without changing your schedule dramatically, and if you're brave enough to ask for help, you're in a good place.

Finally, take your Middle Goal and make it even smaller by turning it into an Easy Goal that

1. Has a short time frame (one to seven days)
2. Has obvious first steps
3. Is not expensive
4. Is fun
5. Is so small it feels like "not enough"

If you can apply for three jobs this week, if you can find a few used cars online that eventually might fit your needs, if you can work close to home so it doesn't cost you too much gas money to get there, if you have fun in the process, and if you feel like you should be doing more, you've got a great Easy Goal.

When you go back down the goal ladder like that, you've just accomplished what 99 percent of people fail to do.

You've taken a big game and made it actionable.

You took *someday* and translated it into *today*.

You escaped the Comfort Zone, avoided the Chaos Zone, and took your first steps into the Potential Zone.

You figured out how teens win.

You're no longer part of the 50 percent of people

who feel they're leaving 50 percent of their potential untapped.

You're opening all your Christmas presents, not just half.

And McRae and I can't wait to see what you do with them!

ACKNOWLEDGMENTS

From McRae

Baker Books, we did it again! Thanks for continuing to show me how fun it is to publish books. Thank you, Brian Vos, for steering this idea from start to finish. Thank you to all the teachers who taught me how teens win, specifically Mrs. Hollingsworth, Mr. Crafton, Mrs. Butler, and Mrs. Castle. Above all, thank you for reading this book! I love seeing your posts on Instagram and am so grateful for the support.

From L.E.

Baker Books, thank you for another wonderful experience. Brian Vos, your edits were fantastic, and Laura Powell, you knocked it out of the park with that cover! I knew the minute I saw it that it was the one. Mom and Dad, thank you for show-ing me that if you want to accomplish a huge goal like writing a book, you just break it into small easy goals and get started. Thank you to every parent who snuck a $20 bill in the back of *Your New Playlist* to encourage their kids to read. I hope you have one more handy for this book!

From Jon

Writing a book with my kids was like a yearlong take-your-kids-to-work experience. They still don't think I'm cool, but this was definitely a step in the right direction! Thank you to every parent and teacher who read *Your New Playlist* and made this second book possible.

Brian Vos, every time you send back edits I think, "I can't believe I get to do this for a job!" Thanks for constantly sharing your wisdom. Amy Nemecek, William Overbeeke, Eileen Hanson, Olivia Peitsch, Holly Scheevel, and Nathan Henrion and the sales team, thanks for being such wonderful partners. Mike Salisbury and Curtis Yates, this makes six books together! Let's do a whole lot more.

Last but never least, Jenny: you're not technically an author, but let's be honest—any written word that leaves this house is just a riff on something smart you've said in the kitchen. I love you!

NOTES

Chapter 11 Escape the Comfort Zone with an Easy Goal

1. Dan Diamond, "Just 8% of People Achieve Their New Year's Resolutions. Here's How They Do It," *Forbes*, January 1, 2013, https://www.forbes.com/sites/dandiamond/2013/01/01/just-8-of-people-achieve-their-new-years-resolutions-heres-how-they-did-it/?sh=5731defe596b.

Chapter 12 The Ladder Starts Here

1. Jeffery J. Downs and Jami L. Downs, *Streaking: The Simple Practice of Conscious, Consistent Actions That Create Life-Changing Results* (n.p.: Page Two Books, 2020), 38.

Chapter 15 Achieve the Best Kind of Accomplishment

1. "Reinvent Your Life, Raise Millions of Dollars, Do Work That Matters: The Scott Harrison Story," *All It Takes Is a Goal* (podcast), episode 71, May 2, 2022, https://podcasts.apple.com/us/podcast/atg-71-reinvent-your-life-raise-millions-of-dollars/id1547078080?i=1000559295402.

Chapter 16 Joy Is a Fuel

1. Brendan Leonard, *I Hate Running and You Can Too: How to Get Started, Keep Going, and Make Sense of an Irrational Passion* (New York: Artisan Books, 2021), 56.

Chapter 17 Turns Out, It Does Take a Village

1. U.S. Department of Health and Human Services, "New Surgeon General Advisory Raises Alarm about the Devastating Impact of the Epidemic of Loneliness and Isolation in the United States," press release, May 3, 2023, https://www.hhs.gov /about/news/2023/05/03/new-surgeon-general-advisory-raises -alarm-about-devastating-impact-epidemic-loneliness-isolation -united-states.html.

Jon Acuff is the *New York Times* bestselling author of 10 books, including *Soundtracks: The Surprising Solution to Overthinking* and the *Wall Street Journal* #1 bestseller *Finish: Give Yourself the Gift of Done.* When he's not writing or recording his popular podcast, *All It Takes Is a Goal*, Acuff can be found on a stage as one of INC's Top 100 Leadership Speakers. He's spoken to hundreds of thousands of people at conferences, colleges, and companies around the world, including FedEx, Range Rover, Microsoft, Nokia, and Comedy Central. Known for his insights wrapped in humor, Acuff's fresh perspective on life has given him the opportunity to write for *Fast*

Company, the *Harvard Business Review*, and *Time* magazine. Jon lives outside of Nashville, Tennessee, with his wife, Jenny, and two daughters, the authors L.E. and McRae. To learn more, visit JonAcuff.com.

L.E. Acuff is a junior at Samford University in Birmingham, Alabama. In addition to writing books, she loves skimboarding, Frisbee, and skiing. When she's not behind a laptop, she's creating clothing at her sewing machine or music at her piano.

McRae Acuff is a freshman at Samford University in Birmingham, Alabama. She runs cross-country, teaches art at an after-school program, and is somewhere babysitting right now. She's a writer at heart and will probably write the follow-up to *How Teens Win* all by herself.

Soundtracks

The Surprising Solution to Overthinking

Wall Street Journal bestseller

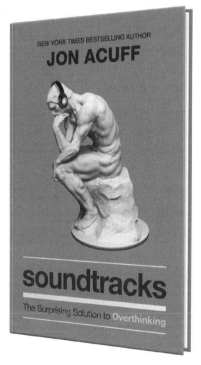

Overthinking isn't a personality trait. It's the sneakiest form of fear.

It steals time, creativity, and goals. It's the most expensive, least productive thing companies invest in without even knowing it. And it's an epidemic.

In *Soundtracks*, *New York Times* bestselling author Jon Acuff offers a proven plan to change overthinking from a super problem into a superpower.

When we don't control our thoughts, our thoughts control us. If our days are full of broken soundtracks, thoughts are our worst enemy, holding us back from the things we really want. But the solution to overthinking isn't to stop thinking. The solution is running our brains with better soundtracks. Once we learn how to choose our soundtracks, thoughts become our best friend, propelling us toward our goals.

If you want to tap into the surprising power of overthinking and give your dreams more time and creativity, learn how to DJ the soundtracks that define you. If you can worry, you can wonder. If you can doubt, you can dominate. If you can spin, you can soar.

Each week, join Jon and guests to explore the best tips, tricks, and techniques to get from where you are today to where you want to be tomorrow. The future belongs to finishers, and this podcast is going to teach you how to be one. All it takes is a goal.

Listen and subscribe at **AllItTakesIsAGoal.com**

BIG LIVES START WITH BIG THOUGHTS.

Create Yours with the *Soundtracks* Course from Jon Acuff!

Jon walks you through six compelling videos full of activities, exercises, and insights that will help you make the most of your time, creativity, and productivity.

LEARN HOW TO

1. Get more done by turning up the music on every important project.

2. Make faster, smarter decisions with the flip of a coin.

3. Accomplish more goals by beating your pocket jury.

4. Improve relationships by picking the right soundtrack for the right person.

5. Create symbols and turn-down techniques that will make new soundtracks stick.

In addition to exclusive content, you'll get a beautiful workbook to guide you each step of the way.

Watch the free trailer at SoundtracksCourse.com!

TRY THIS!

NEWSLETTER BY J🔆N ACUFF

Every two weeks, you'll receive tactical, practical, and surprisingly fun ideas to help you achieve any goal you care about. From parenting tips to techniques to avoid overthinking, procrastination, and perfectionism, you'll love this lightning-fast read from Jon.

Join more than 90,000 high performers already taking actionable steps to achieve their goals.

Sign up today at JonAcuff.com/Newsletter

THE 3-STEP PLAN TO DITCH REGRET AND TAP INTO YOUR MASSIVE POTENTIAL

When *New York Times* bestselling author Jon Acuff got curious about tapping into his full potential, he launched a research study with Dr. Mike Peasley. They asked more than three thousand people if they felt they were living up to their full potential.

Fifty percent of people reported that 50 percent of their full potential is untapped. That means half of us are walking around with half-lives. No wonder Twitter is so grumpy.

Imagine if every Christmas you only opened up half your gifts. You could see the rest—a whole pile of them in the corner of the room—but you never got to open them.

Would that make for a happy Christmas, a happy house, a happy job, a happy anything?

It wouldn't, but what if it didn't have to be that way? What if you could have a fulfilling career? What if you could enjoy a thriving marriage and strong friendships? What if you could be in the greatest shape of your life? What if each day felt like a gift and each year progressively got better? What if you could use a single piece of paper to learn from your past, enjoy your present, and prepare your future? What if you could escape the Comfort Zone, avoid the Chaos Zone, and live in the Potential Zone? That would be the best.

And what if all it takes is a goal?

Pick up a copy of All It Takes Is a Goal *anywhere books are sold, or read the first chapter for free at AllItTakesIsAGoalBook.com.*